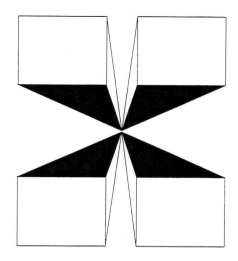

WHAT IF THEY DON'T RESPOND?

Four Approaches To
Influencing People With STYLE

David L. Teske

Stevens, Foster Publishing

Dedication

*This book is dedicated to all those in my personal
and professional life who taught me STYLE.*

Your patience, insight, skill...

*and just **your being you** helped me greatly.*

Thank you

Printed in the United States of America.
J I H G F E D C B A

Address orders and inquiries to:

Stevens, Foster Publishing
8500 Normandale Lake Boulevard, Suite 140
Bloomington, MN 55437
(612) 921-3982 • Fax (612) 921-8369 • (800) 678-5558

Contents

Please note: The author has attempted to equalize gender pronouns throughout the book.

Foreword

As a recognition driven, *Tell Assertive Expressive*, I was delighted when I was asked by Dave Teske's publisher to comment on his book.

In the great atom smasher of life, the high energy world of commerce bombards the ever fluxing world of social communication. Generated by these magnificent collisions are an almost infinite range of possibilities. Rarely do these comings together not necessitate a search for new means to negotiate the pathways created by their meetings. Out of these interactions, entrepreneurs hope to find new markets, competitive advantage, and wealth. Out of this dynamically propelled and uncontrolled evolution (occasionally revolution), individuals hope to find personal growth, meaningful relationships, and self-actualization. The world of commerce and the world of social communication meet on the vast, and only partially explored plain called *Communication*. Searchers for synergies are we one and all. Pretentious as these words may sound, a particle of truth may be found in their hyperbole.

"The hardest things to do are to manage people and machines!" This insight was shared with me by a computer operator. He was one of the first people I supervised at the beginning of my career. He confided his wisdom to me after we had worked fruitlessly into the night in an attempt to get a computer functioning in the middle of a holiday weekend. Struggling with service personnel and test equipment, we had little success. Getting the vendor's service personnel to understand our plight, or for that matter getting the test equipment to function, appeared to be similar to landing on the shores of a distant planet without the necessary travel guides and dictionaries. Communication was not a happening thing!

Since then I have added *money* to the computer operator's list of *hardest things to manage*. Over the years his words rang truer with each new management communication challenge. One day I realized that it wasn't just the world of business that was the problem here (or is it *hear?*) The problem included all life situations which required interacting with other people. The main medium of this interaction was some type of communication. Not much that happens in one's life, which is meaningful, is therefore excluded from the wise old computer operator's insight.

And then along came Dave.

Trudge on dear reader. The journey is simpler with the right maps; the journey to understanding is easier than we might fear.

For me, David's work has served as the travel guide and dictionary which facilitates interpersonal communication on the many shores of this planet. From the company I manage, to my daily interactions with people, and through my interpersonal relationships with significant others, David's ideas and insights have improved my overall effectiveness and ability to get things done through people. I have learned to do this while enabling my psychological *comforts and needs* to be met. At the same time, I learned to minimize interpersonal conflicts. The key to this, for me, was to make a conscious effort to improve my interpersonal Flexibility and to diligently apply Dave's *LSQPA* technique.

We have established using STYLE and *LSQPA* as part of our cultural platform in the company I manage. It has been in use now for over 12 years. One of the sources, many of my management team believe, of our competitive advantage in the marketplace is our use of these tools in working with our internal and external customers. Every member of our management team has been through this course. We encourage our production personnel to become cognizant of STYLE and *LSQPA* techniques so they can more effectively communicate with one another and management. We let everyone who goes through STYLE training at work know that it is a valuable tool for use in their private life as well.

As we move forward in our commitment to continuously improve our business, we believe it is essential that our employees also continuously improve in their ability to communicate and raise their level of Flexibility. Our future capacity to effectively compete will always be grounded in the creativity, skills, and communication practices of our people. Their STYLE and the STYLE of our organization will shape our competence in winning and retaining customers.

On the personal side, my two teenage children have become effective practitioners of STYLE. My son, who is studying to be a teacher of multiply challenged children, uses it in the classroom. My daughter has used STYLE to analyze characters in literature and as part of her arsenal of tools on the debate team. What is important is that they, their peers, and their teachers believe that they are communicating more effectively since studying with Dave.

Dave's book celebrates the richness and diversity of human behavior. He cuts through to the core elements which characterize how people negotiate the world. Dave shares with us his insights about how people try to achieve their own comforts and satisfaction through their STYLE of communication. In so doing, he teaches us how to more meaningfully communicate with all types of individuals for our mutual gratification. That is relationship synergy at its best.

Neil A. Levy
September 1995

(Editor's note. For more information about Neil A. Levy, see the *Advisors List* in the Appendices.)

Preface

WHY LEARN TO UNDERSTAND STYLE?

"This Book Is About Being More Effective With People."

Most will find something of value here.

> Most of us want someone else to respond in some way. If we manage others we want them to respond productively. If we sell, we want our customers to respond by buying. If we have a troubled relationship with a significant other, our children, or our boss we want the other to respond in a manner which gives us what we want.
>
> A knowledge and practice of STYLE can help as *it offers significant insight to facilitating results in important relationships with others.*

FOR THOSE WHO ARE NEW TO STYLE

This material is written to be read by individuals who have not been exposed to STYLE before. For this reason an effort has been made to explain technical concepts without detailed clinical definitions.

FOR EXPERIENCED PRACTITIONERS OF STYLE

Those who are *STYLE literate* are likely to find value in a new perspective. When I attend meetings of my peers in training and development and the subject of STYLE arises, some speak of it from their reference of having been exposed through one seminar, or workshop—or through association with one company or organization.

There are dozens of organizations (six of which I have studied with extensively) that have conducted STYLE research and have something unique to add to our knowledge base. When I hear someone from the training or consulting community dismiss STYLE because they have *had it,* I wonder if their frame of reference is from one or two sources. When I dig a little deeper with them, I find this to be true much of the time.

Having taken a STYLE seminar once, or even twice is like having a hot dog and saying you know what meat is. Even though the hot dog is very good and effectively satisfies a need, it gives you very little understanding of the broad, rich selection available.

One of my associates of twelve years, now a corporate executive with an extensive knowledge of STYLE, said to me on discussing this introduction: "I tell my people who may have been exposed to STYLE before taking the internal seminar we offer—don't think you know it all. If you took a seminar on how to do your taxes, you wouldn't then know the field of accounting." She is right, and I hadn't thought of this analogy.

There is a tremendous and exciting world of additional discovery concerning STYLE and more yet to be learned.

In this work there are a number of conjectures and points contributed by others which may give new insight to this marvelous technology, and certainly contribute to the base knowledge of the new learner. Please see the advisor list in the Appendix to read about those who leant their knowledge and expertise.

> **This book is for individuals who want to more effectively work with others—enhancing important relationships and adding to their success with people.**

THIS BOOK IS DESIGNED TO BUILD SKILL IN INFLUENCING:

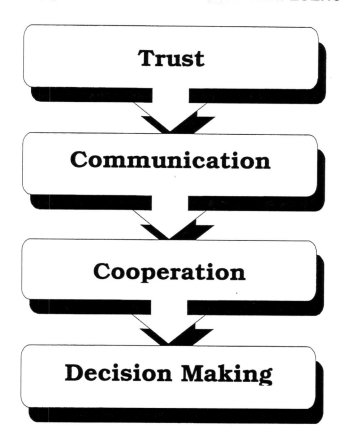

That's a lot. In case you wish to have more specifics, here are some additional ideas:

WHAT IF THEY DON'T RESPOND? can assist trainers—who wish to have a text for their interpersonal communication contributing to team building, sales training, leadership/management, and conflict resolution.

Managers leading a Total Quality initiative, or creating self directed/self managing teams who want to facilitate communication and cooperation insuring the success of the effort, may find STYLE useful as a core training element for employees to understand and work well with each other.

Consultants may wish to use it as a resource to improve their client's interpersonal effectiveness, thus making the consultant's job easier.

Salespeople who wish to understand their customers better will find STYLE knowledge helps to make more sales.

Parents will find insight to their children's behavior, and both will learn more about the business of living with others, thus making parenting less frustrating and more effective.

Those who wish to grow and gain in knowledge and ability to affect a better life with significant others, their boss, their peers, or any important relationship will find something of value in understanding STYLE.

Finally, **WHAT IF THEY DON'T RESPOND?** *is designed to be an uncomplicated introduction to understanding the basic principles of STYLE.* This information is designed to be used ***immediately***.

Did I cover everyone? Yes, I think I did.

David L. Teske
September 1995

STYLEBYTE

I am an Expressive, so I need an additional word or two in this introduction. (You will discover what an Expressive is shortly, if you haven't heard yet.)

At the conclusion of each chapter will be a **STYLEBYTE** of information. These are attempts to summarize through example a main point in the chapter. Some STYLEBYTES may be humorous, and some direct, but all are written with the goal in mind to give you an additional thought or example.

This extra thought at chapter end may contribute greatly to your *application* of STYLE.

Here is your first STYLEBYTE.

When I was a kid, I read a science fiction story in which a secret formula was contrived to predict how people were going to act. What a great power, I thought. If you wanted someone to do something for you, all you had to do was apply the special formula and bingo! They did it. Visions of candy store doors being opened at my command danced in my head.

Would be nice, wouldn't it? Well, although it doesn't work as snappy as in science fiction, *there is a Formula*. It can predict with some accuracy how others *may* act. It will also give you guidance in influencing trust, and thus influencing communication, cooperation, and decision making.

Want more about the Secret Formula? Read Chapter One.

THE SECRET FORMULA

"We May Be Misunderstood...
We May Misunderstand Others"

Sometimes it seems when we think we have someone figured out, they do something differently just to let us know people can still be a mystery.

STYLE

STYLE—the Secret Formula—really isn't a secret. It has been available for centuries, most notably in history through the "Four Temperaments" from the Middle Ages. This was the method which divided people into four types based upon what was believed then to be a predominant *humor*, or inner juice. As ridiculous sounding as this is, the *descriptions* generated for the four humors of Choleric, Sanguine, Melancholic and Phlegmatic are remarkably like the modern counterparts of **Driver, Expressive, Amiable, and Analytical.**

In more modern times research in this area was conducted by Carl Jung who published *Psychological Types* in 1921.

> **The *Secret Formula...understanding the STYLE of others...*will give you more opportunity for compassion and understanding of people to help them, and be helped by them.**

Later, we will review detail of STYLE...but for now...

> **STYLE is basically a mixture of habits and conditioning which are comfortable for us and we exhibit these through our behaviors.**

What this means is we all have comfortable ways of behaving. For example, some of us are talkative, so when we chatter away it is a comfortable behavior. Some people like to be more quiet and speak only after much deliberation. This behavior is then comfortable for these people. We have many, many more behaviors and the human list is too numerous for this book.

We have developed these behaviors over time and they have become habits integrated in our way of living life and reacting to others. We may not be aware of many of them.

> **This *behavior bundle* forms what others see of us, and what they see is called our STYLE.**

There is some debate as to whether STYLE behaviors are learned or inherited. At the time this book went to press, there has been little proof submitted one way or another. We do know, however, the behaviors that make up STYLE can be witnessed observing a child in the crib.

In the last fifty years STYLE technology has been applied to counseling, parenting, selling, managing, and many other legitimate applications where understanding the motivations and behaviors of others is essential. Through additional research by the many persons and organizations actively using STYLE we have learned a great deal about working with it in the last five years.

I'm going to share with you what I have learned about STYLE technology from various resources, including the companies I studied from, and the persons and organizations listed in the Appendix as "Advisors".

WHY A TECHNOLOGY?

We call this STYLE *technology* because there is application of some very well researched principles which are scientific in nature. Softer science than, let's say industrial engineering, but science non-the-less. The bottom line is we can apply these principles, or methods and expect certain outcomes personally, (such as in a better relationship) or commercially, (such as in more productive sales, or as in motivating employees to produce at a higher level).

Among its many labels STYLE is called **Interpersonal Behavior Technology, Behavioral Style, Social Style, or Personality Types.** Perhaps you have heard the terms—**Analytical, Driver, Amiable, and Expressive**—or similar labels.

There have been many behavior *typing* seminars, programs, and books in which behaviors of individuals are studied in an attempt to understand more about the person. This is called TYPING. These sources deal with understanding yourself and others by the habits you have and the behaviors you display.

In this work we will look at *your* STYLE, and that of others, to see how it can add to the quality and success of important relationships in your career and life in general.

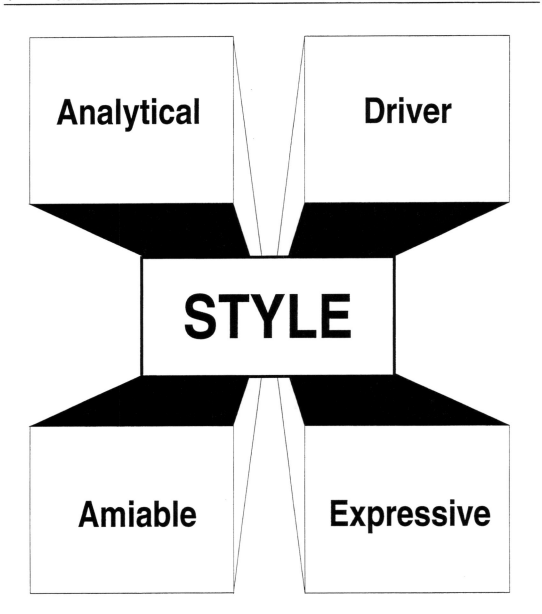

PEOPLE PROBLEMS / OPPORTUNITIES

As you read the following statements, think of things said by those around you from time to time.

"I'm just not comfortable with him."

"She's so quiet, I don't know if I'm getting through to her."

"All he wants is more information. No matter what I do, I can't please him."

"She's too flighty. I don't think she'll make a good decision."

"Pushy; he's just too pushy."

"She just doesn't care about the people side of things."

"I wouldn't want him for an employee, even if I got him."

And on, and on, and on ...

JUDGEMENTS

The previous quotes represent *people problems*. They express the kinds of problems that get in the way of coworkers, customer service, sales, management, marriage...relationships of all kinds. Judgements may also get in the way of helping, or gaining the co-operation of your peers, associates, customers or significant others. Here's how:

The emotional perceptions (or feelings) formed as a result of correct or incorrect observations may cause us to form inaccurate JUDGEMENTS of others.

These emotional perceptions work the other way too. Others may judge us and decide we are not worth communicating, or cooperating with!

Usually, these judgements are incorrect if they are a reaction to the STYLE, and not to the real or actual *quality* of intelligence, competency, or *intent* of the person. We witness the STYLE and our feelings judge the person. We may not be seeing the real person at all, just how we *feel* based upon a limited amount of information.

Judgements may sound like:

"They're incompetent."

She's not smart enough."

"I don't trust him."

STYLE DIFFERENCES

STYLE Differences affect us. They may cause us to judge the person incorrectly...and because of that we miss out. We may miss out by losing potentially good workers, good associates, customers...even good friends and significant others. We may also not receive maximum productivity from those who stay with us.

STYLE Differences influence us, and others...and this happens quite often because our STYLE is always with us and always part of human interaction.

Some of our feelings about others may be the result of STYLE Differences and may be totally inaccurate.

Remember our quick definition of STYLE...

STYLE is a mixture of habits and conditioning, exhibited through behaviors that affect our comfort.

STYLE, because it is exhibited as a behavior, influences us to form judgements of others...and they of us.

Quick example? Some people have **personal comforts** such as the need to take their time in making decisions. These can influence some people to seek a great deal of information about a given subject. Detailed information. This **personal comfort need** lengthens their decision making process.

To someone else, one who has a **comfort need** to make quick decisions, the above behavior may be *perceived* as not cooperating, or not being satisfied. This may be frustrating to the person who wants to move more quickly.

So, who's right? They both are. They both have different ways of dealing with a given task which may give equal results. In fact, under some conditions, the person who wants the detail may make the better decision...under another set of circumstances the person who is comfortable moving faster may make the better decision...but both are right based upon the behaviors with which they are comfortable.

WAIT?   DECIDE?
Both believe it's the right decision.
Both may be a right decision!

STYLE CONFLICT

In the meantime, the people in our example may be defeating the opportunity to work together because they don't understand each other's STYLE and that conflict in STYLE can negate success.

STYLE Conflict happens in management, sales, counseling, marriages, customer relations, work groups, parenting...even global politics.

Even when it is understood, STYLE can't be changed easily. Many people spend high amounts of energy in conflict or trying to *change* STYLE Differences. An example would be trying to make someone else do something your way, even though their way would obtain similar results. Instead, the energy and time could be better spent on understanding what the other person needs for their comfort, and then contributing to that comfort.

Different STYLES are not wrong, just different.

History gives us an excellent example of this. General Eisenhower, the Supreme Allied Commander during the Second World War, worked with some very dynamic people labeled by historians as strong willed or even *difficult.* General Patton, Field Marshall Montgomery, Churchill, De Gaulle, Roosevelt—all were very direct and determined in getting their way. What Eisenhower did was not compete directly with these competitive behaviors (STYLE type behaviors), but allowed these individuals to speak their minds. He listened to them, which was not competing, and then he would decide, independently, what to do.

By letting them speak their mind, he was not trying to change their STYLE—i.e. making them listen to him. Later, he could be very convincing in presenting his ideas and gained their cooperation much of the time because *they had a sense he had heard them.* By listening he obtained broad results, still made his own decisions and provided the leadership which won the war in Europe.

> **Helping the other person feel comfortable is usually a more productive answer—*and accomplished in much less time—than trying to change the other person's* STYLE. It is also the way to influence the person to cooperate with you.**

WHAT IS STYLE TRAINING?

STYLE Training is designed to give a better understanding of others—how to work with their STYLE, and get better results in many important aspects of career and life.

So, how do you work the formula and gain cooperation? This book will help to answer that question. It is also designed to promote the idea that there are different ways of achieving success and the **Differences** can lead to better results.

FLEXIBILITY

Understanding **FLEXIBILITY**—a skill that helps us recognize and use the **DIFFERENCES** for effective results—is the goal of this material. Instead of fighting the **Differences** we believe in *CELEBRATING THE DIFFERENCES.*

One way to master effective STYLE application is through understanding our Flexibility or versatility with others.

Using Flexibility in appropriate situations is a major reason to study STYLE. Our ability to be flexible in communication is one way we can cope better with others, and how we influence them.

The Eisenhower example is *one example* of Flexibility.
—*The timing of when he listened and when he presented*
—*The patience to wait*
—*The ability to decide and powerfully present his point*

All are examples of his Flexibility strength.

STYLE MAPS

Also, you can chart the comforts, or behavior **Differences**. The references to maps and charts refer to the mapping of behavior or comfort zones. To *CELEBRATE THE DIFFERENCES*, a person must know where to look for them. The **STYLE Maps** will help.

On page five, you were asked to think about the statements presented in terms of what may have been said about others. Think of a situation where things didn't go as well interpersonally as you wished...could any of the situations described in these statements been a STYLE factor?

> We will discuss many behaviors and interpersonal habits in this book. We will also be covering ways to effectively work with others in difficult situations. *Understanding STYLE is a shorthand to knowing and doing these things.* If we understand the STYLE of others, many ways of working out solutions to people problems will be apparent.

Later, in the book, we will outline a way for you to determine your own STYLE.

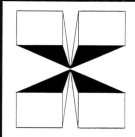

How Do We Get Them To Respond?

We have a greater chance of getting others to respond more positively if we strive to understand, not misunderstand, that their outward STYLE behavior is not necessarily the real person. This helps us to be less judgmental so we treat others with dignity and respect.

At the same time we project a more positive image about ourselves which motivates the other person to treat us in kind.

STYLEBYTE

Many times when I am doing training in interpersonal communication, sales and customer skills, leadership management, or negotiating, the subject matter seems to bring out questions from people who are having conflict with someone in their life.

"He just doesn't give me a chance to say anything." a woman told me one morning. *"I don't know what to do."*

"What does he do?" I asked.

"Whenever I ask about something important to me, he jumps in and cuts me off."

"What do you do then?" I asked.

"I just give up." she said with frustration.

In her case, she is probably dealing with a person whose STYLE is opposite hers in communication. Her STYLE is to "Ask" more and suggest—his is to "Tell" more and direct.

This is a typical example of STYLE Conflict and can be very frustrating to both persons.

It is frustrating to her because she doesn't get her point out, and it is frustrating to him, because he doesn't get any feedback.

She feels that more assertiveness is pushy and so is not comfortable in being more assertive for that and other reasons. She then shuts down when he goes to tell behavior and doesn't push her point more.

He, on the other hand, *may be very comfortable* even if she asserts herself, because he is OK with more of that kind of behavior in communicating.

In order for her to be less frustrated in this, she would need to take his STYLE less personally. In other words be less upset with his behavior because his intention may not be to shut her down and it may not be directed to her personally, but is an aspect of his learned behavior which he is doing unconsciously.

Taking *his* STYLE less personally, and understanding it more, may help her to see that her own behavior when she asserts herself is not inappropriate either.

Then, she needs to assert her points more directly to him. Not attack him, but be a bit more forceful in getting air time.

To do this, she must leave, temporarily, an aspect of her comfort—that of suggesting—and be more directing. Please realize, she is not to change who she is, only understand better the aspects of this situation and temporarily modify some of her behavior to make her point.

Part of her success in making herself heard is dependent on her choice and skill in flexing by temporarily modifying her behavior.

He, on the other hand, to be more successful in communication, needs to listen and check more often with others. This may be as uncomfortable for him to do as directing is for her.

Both, to get more of what they want from others, need to understand the communication aspect of STYLE, and/or focus the energy to do something not part of their present comforts and habits.

We will discuss more of the *whys* of this in the next two chapters, and then get into more of the *hows*.

Chapter Two

ASSERTIVENESS

"We Try To Control Each Other"

Imagine for a moment, you, as a human being were constantly radiating something, or things, which affected others. No, not germs, but intangible messages which affected how others feel about you. Well, we do this. It's called behavior. Behavior here is more than acting *nice*, or *good*—as *being on your best behavior*. It is instead a complex bundle of comforts and habits—preferred ways we do things in life.

If you may have experienced putting your watch on the other wrist, and have then felt it *doesn't feel right* or is *strange*. This is one example of changing a habit, and it is uncomfortable because it is not the preferred way you wear your watch.

RECOGNIZING AND MAPPING STYLE

There has been great debate in behavioral science. Professionals have difficulty agreeing on the different aspects of psychology. One of the few areas of agreement by this community is that people exhibit *bundles of behavior* in two very broad ways, **ASSERTIVENESS** and **REACTIVENESS**.

ASSERTIVENESS

There are many definitions of this word, to be sure. For our purposes, we will use the following definition.

> **ASSERTIVENESS is the degree to which a person attempts to control the thoughts and actions of others.**

Assertiveness is not a *good* or *bad*, *right* or *wrong*. It is only a description of behavior. It may be illustrated by using the following chart:

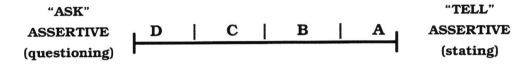

The extremes of this chart illustrate the extremes in **Tell** or **Ask** behavior (Tell and Ask being descriptive of the behavior). An "A" Assertive above, for instance is comfortable in a *stating* mode. In other words, Tell statements are natural as opposed to a "D" Assertive who is more comfortable in a *questioning*, or Asking mode. Figuratively, the "A" Assertive wears the watch on the right, and the "D" on the left. Their habits (and therefore, their comforts) are not the same when it comes to stating or questioning.

Perhaps you know someone who is comfortable in a *stating* mode. They seem to spend more time **Telling** when they communicate. You also may be familiar with someone who predominantly **Asks** you questions when you encounter them.

The preceding examples are the extremes of this behavior. Very few people exhibit predominantly TELL or ASK behavior all the time.

> **Ask or Tell behavior is not right or wrong—no more than there is a right or wrong wrist on which to wear a watch.**
>
> **It represents COMFORT for those displaying it.**
>
> **It is how they communicate.**
>
> **Successful people come from all parts of the Assertiveness chart.**

Most of us may, at times, exhibit behavior from all over the chart. Behavioral science shows us, though, that there is one place, a *home*, which is most comfortable for us. We return to it much of the time.

Where is your *home* on the Assertiveness chart; more Asking than Telling, or more Telling than Asking?

CELEBRATE THE DIFFERENCES

TELL and ASK persons may be in conflict with each other because they misread the behavior **Difference**. The result is missed opportunities and perhaps failure instead of success in a given situation.

> **The more we can accept DIFFERENCE, the less it gets in the way of our dealings with others. In other words, we direct less energy on the things we can't change easily, and direct it to those things we can.**

CELEBRATING THE DIFFERENCES and realizing that the behavior displayed by others may cause a false perception of what the person is really like. This is a more productive decision than choosing to try to change another person or entering into needless conflict with that person.

It may reflect just a Difference in STYLE.

Then, we are more apt to focus on those issues which can affect decision making and influence the other person to trust, communicate, and cooperate with us.

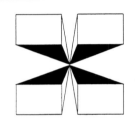

How Do We Get Them To Respond?

If we understand that everyone displays some aspect of either ASK or TELL assertiveness, we will get others to respond by letting them display it. This is comfortable behavior for the other person.

By trying to make TELL ASSERTIVES stop talking, or trying to make ASK ASSERTIVES respond before they are ready, we run the risk of them not wanting to communicate with us at all.

This doesn't mean we do not get a chance to present our view to a TELL, or get an ASK to verbalize. It means we must be patient (an aspect of Flexibility) and *earn the right* to tell a TELL, and ask an ASK.

STYLEBYTE

A True Story In Fairy Tale Form

Once upon a time a few of us in the Great Kingdom of Wisdom believed Assertiveness could be described as *High* and *Low*, as in High Assertive, or Low Assertive. So, we nailed the High label on the right side where Tell is now, and the Low label on the left side where Ask is now.

We supposed that *Asks* were not very assertive and *Tells* were, and some of us felt smug and happy.

We probably thought this great feeling because several of us were *Tells* and wanted to directly get our way on the matter.

Then the *Asks* in our group shut down and wouldn't talk to us, because they didn't agree with us.

No matter how strongly the *Tells* pushed and pushed, the *Asks* continued to shut down and not communicate. They wouldn't even talk to the *Tells* about other things they had to talk about. They wouldn't yell, or talk back, or raise their voices—they would just sit and not teach, or write, or produce, or sell, or even take out the trash.

It was very frustrating for *Tells*. I know because I am one.

We weren't getting our way!

We felt controlled.

Then, some of the smarter ones of us (or was it the more Flexible ones?) said *"Hum, these 'Asks' are being pretty stubborn with us. I guess they aren't Low Assertive after all."*

Then we learned, and eventually we all felt good because we understood one another better.

And because of this we lived more happily afterward.

The End

Both Asks and Tells can be highly Assertive. Perhaps you have experienced customers, coworkers, and (gasp) even significant others *Shut Down* until they get their way.

I have seen senior executives Shut Down decision making—which has Shut Down entire companies and organizations until they were ready to make a decision.

Shutting Down isn't the only assertive behavior for Asks—there are many, but it is a very powerful one!

Chapter Three

REACTIVENESS

"The Light And Shadow Of Emotions And Feelings"

The other dimension of behavior is **REACTIVENESS**, which has also been termed Objectivity or Responsiveness. It pertains to the outward demonstration, or lack of, displayed emotion.

> **REACTIVENESS is the degree a person tends to control the outward expression of feelings, responses, and emotions.**

Again, Reactiveness is not *right* or *wrong* behavior, it is a description of behavior, and illustrates a different dimension than Assertiveness.

Reactiveness is illustrated by the chart on the following page. The Reactiveness Scale illustrates the extremes in behavior. An individual who is comfortable showing little or no expression, feelings, or emotion is a low-Reactive, who **Controls** outward expression of emotions, and may be at "1" on the Scale. This individual may be the *poker faced* person whose expressions don't change greatly.

It is important to *CELEBRATE THE DIFFERENCES* here and realize these persons have all the emotions and feelings of any human being, but will feel mild to great discomfort in showing these emotions.

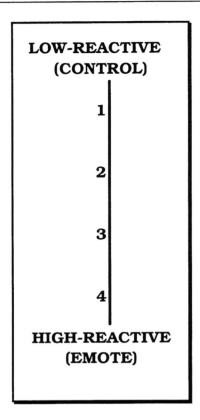

REACTIVENESS SCALE

This **Control Reactive** person described on the last page *may be misread* as being non-caring, aloof, unfriendly to persons showing emotions in positions 3 or 4. This illustrates a STYLE Conflict and may not be the reality of the person at all.

An individual who is comfortable in showing emotions, feelings, and expression is more Reactive, sometimes labeled as **Emote** and may be at 3 or 4 on the Scale.

These people may be misread at times as being *too emotional*. The **Difference** to be celebrated here, once again, is that the above judgements may not represent the true person at all...just an outward display of behavior.

> **Again...these are dimensions of behavior and are not indicators of intelligence, success, knowledge, or of being right or wrong. They are components of someone's STYLE.**

In terms of Reactiveness, where on the Scale is your *home*? Where are you most comfortable?

AN IMPORTANT POINT ABOUT THE CHARTS

Many times we human beings see behavior that is different than ours and judge the **Differences** as wrong. We are not comfortable with the outward behavior. We may, because of the Difference, assign other negative traits such as low intelligence, low trust, or incompetence.

> **Intelligence, character, success potential, goodness, or badness are not shown by the outward behavior of ASSERTIVENESS or REACTIVENESS.**

People may indeed be competent or incompetent, trustworthy or untrustworthy...but *behavioral **STYLE** does not show those things. Qualities or negatives must be assessed beyond STYLE...not based upon the STYLE.*

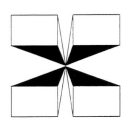

How Do We
Get Them To Respond?

Reactiveness is a result of behavior which is comfortable for that person. We stand a better chance of getting others to respond if we allow them to be CONTROL REACTIVE, or EMOTE REACTIVE. By trying to get a CONTROL to EMOTE, or an EMOTE to be more CONTROLLED, we are making them unnecessarily uncomfortable.

If we want them to respond to us, we must be patient and let them respond in the manner right for them. Not remake them, even if the behavior is uncomfortable to us.

STYLEBYTE

We humans invent much when it comes to Reactiveness. We observe the Reactive behavior and make assumptions about it inventing intentions, character, morals, competency—when these and many other aspects of the inner person cannot be known by witnessing Reactive behaviors alone.

Because we sometimes don't take the time to know the real person, some of us through our imagination, build Frankenstein monsters, as well as guardian angels—many times I have witnessed both creations to be completely false.

If we are very sensitive in our feelings, or insecure in ourselves, our perception of Reactiveness can become very exaggerated. One such situation was when a young woman told me she was convinced her manager didn't care about her, as the manager was so *impersonal* that "she couldn't possibly feel anything for me". I knew her manager. The manager, another woman, was Control Reactive. This woman was achievement-oriented and on task in her career and life.

Quite unaware of her employee's feelings about her, she had great empathy for the worker. The manager told me how hard it must be for the younger woman to have nice things at this stage in her career.

She wanted to give the employee an inexpensive fur coat she no longer needed. The coat meant much to the manager as it symbolized for her a sense of accomplishment in life when she had been about the same age as her employee.

I knew this manager well, and the gesture was not meant to be condescending, or superior. It was an honest attempt to show understanding and to help another human being. She decided not to give the coat, however, thinking it might be misunderstood.

Instead she supported the employee by coaching her into tasks and positions of more responsibility—helping her career. The gesture was received with suspicion and contempt. The employee talked about it to her friends and used it as a means of further *evidence* the manager really didn't care— she said the manager was treating her as an inferior—forcing her to do more work.

There were other factors at work here, of course. The employee had other emotional problems or perceptions and not all of them were STYLE related. The misread of Reactiveness, however, only made the situation worse for the employee, most notably that once she formed her opinion of the manager she didn't accept the reality of the inner person.

Many of our inventions have nothing to do with the real person—they may form perceptions based on the expression of emotion, or lack thereof in the other person.

This has equated to highly qualified Emotes not being hired by Control managers because they seemed *too* emotional, or even *flaky*.

It has surfaced by Emote salespeople feeling Control customers *just don't like them* so the salesperson stops calling on the customer and loses business.

Emote and Control parents have worried needlessly about their opposite Reactive children because they seemed *different* but were otherwise well-adjusted for their age.

If any of the events in the previous illustration have happened to you, whether you are the *misreader* or the *misread*, it is time to pay attention to the real person *inside* the Reactive behavior. This may mean understanding more about how you judge others, or how others may be judging you based upon this dimension of STYLE.

Chapter Four

THE STYLE MAP

"There Are No Wrong STYLES"

HOW TO CHART BASIC BEHAVIOR

Assertiveness and Reactiveness behaviors are like latitude and longitude on a map. They intersect and a behavior, or **STYLE Map,** is formed. With it we can chart basic behavior.

This chart can help us understand STYLE more effectively.

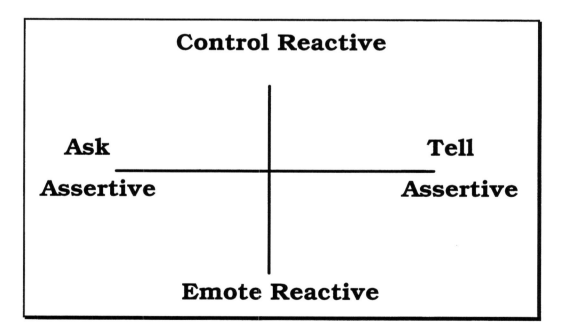

The STYLE Map

The Map now plots specific behavioral dimensions, and we can then label the parts with terms that describe combinations of behavior and comfort based upon Assertiveness and Reactiveness as a starting point.

Control Reactive

ANALYTICAL	**DRIVER**
Ask Assertive	**Tell Assertive**
AMIABLE	**EXPRESSIVE**

Emote Reactive

THE TERMS ARE ONLY LABELS

The terms—**Analytical, Driver, Expressive, and Amiable**—are **STYLE Labels** which make understanding of STYLE easier. Here is a brief, technical description of each STYLE:

ANALYTICAL	**Control Reactive** and **Ask Assertive**
DRIVER	**Control Reactive** and **Tell Assertive**
EXPRESSIVE	**Emote Reactive** and **Tell Assertive**
AMIABLE	**Emote Reactive** and **Ask Assertive**

Or, perhaps the following diagram helps you visualize this description.

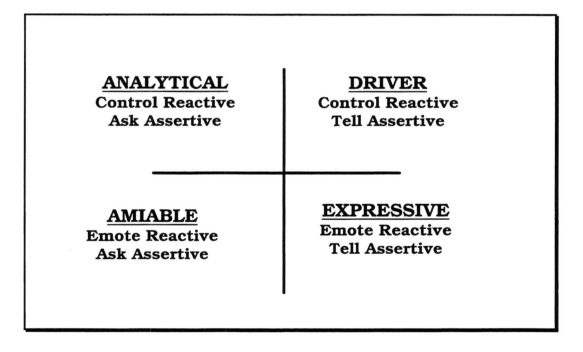

Studies by many companies involved with STYLE technology have shown very successful men and women of each STYLE.

> **All STYLES are right for the people who have them. In other words, there is no wrong, or bad STYLE. Each is not a designation of intelligence, success, or knowledge. They are an illustration of comforts and represent Differences to be celebrated.**

STYLE DETAIL

Each person is unique...and it is very difficult to put people in neat little boxes characterizing them exactly. **STYLE Technology** shows we all have some preferences and behaviors in common. It also shows there are certain ways we are uniquely different. Understanding this and practicing interpersonal skills based on STYLE Technology is a way to more readily lower tension and gain trust, communication, and cooperation—which lead to business success, sales, friendship, more successful parenting, or many other interpersonal goals.

STYLE QUICK REFERENCE MAP

Here it is—the Formula—which also shows that *certain something* we radiate. The following STYLE Map is meant as a guide in helping you understand comfort preferences of different STYLES. The information in parenthesis ( ) indicates a major personal need of that STYLE. The characteristics listed are those that are generally perceived to be accurate for that STYLE.

ANALYTICAL **(being right)** fact oriented, businesslike, independent but cooperative, cool, uncommunicative, usually likes dealing in detail, engineers risk from decisions, does- n't like to be uncertain	**DRIVER** **(being in control)** direct, fact oriented, cool and independent, business like, fast to act and make decisions, com- petitive, initiates action, doesn't like to be slowed down, wants to know the bottom line
AMIABLE **(being secure)** feeling oriented, communicative, warm, cooperative, supportive, people oriented, minimizes risk, slow actions and decision making, doesn't like to be pushed into action	**EXPRESSIVE** **(being recognized)** communicative, warm, feeling oriented, approachable, risk taker, competitive, makes fast decisions and actions, doesn't like detail, excitable, a dreamer and wants others to listen

INTERPRETING THE QUICK REFERENCE MAP

This Map shows the four basic STYLES. Based on the Map, each STYLE shares some characteristics of other STYLES. It is also important to note that this description is a composite...meaning not all Analyticals or Expressives, etc....show all characteristics listed on the Quick Reference Map all of the time.

Human beings are unique, so they refuse to *fit the mold*. We all have, however, a place where we are most comfortable to be, our *home*, and we will return to that place or STYLE.

Where do your Reactive and Assertive *homes* intersect? This intersection will give you some idea of your major STYLE.

SUBQUADRANTS

Each major quadrant of STYLE may be broken down again forming a map within a map. There are many variations of each STYLE which explains why there seems to be different Drivers, or Amiables, etc.

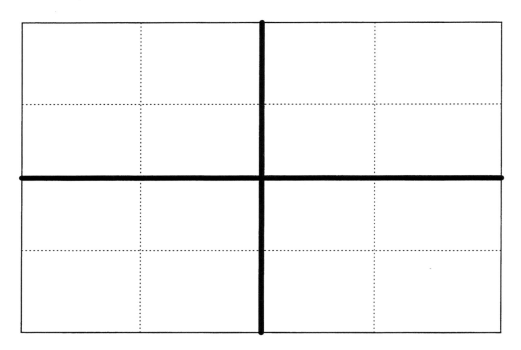

WHAT IS STYLE?—A SUMMARY

- Main dimensions of STYLE are Assertiveness and Reactiveness.
- These dimensions are a description of comfort and behaviors. They do not indicate intelligence, success, morals, or skill.
- Comfort, or behavior needs can change, but like comfortable clothes are something we give up slowly, if ever, and then under pressure to change.
- STYLE can be broken down into Subquadrants and this illustrates why there are variations of each STYLE.

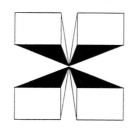

How Do We
Get Them To Respond?

There are no wrong STYLES—only STYLES that are different than our own. We may not be totally comfortable with all STYLE behaviors. If we react to someone's STYLE negatively, we run the risk of them sensing it and then not wanting to respond in the manner we want.

If we let others be their STYLE, the chance is greater they will be more accepting of our own...which may be equally uncomfortable to them.

STYLEBYTE

DENIAL

The vast majority of people when they participate in a STYLE seminar see STYLE as real and understand their own STYLE very quickly.

Sometimes though, some people DENY they have a STYLE. They say things like *"I see myself all over the map; I'm just not one STYLE."* or, *"I don't know about this STYLE thing, I just don't see how you can say this about people."*

One way to define denial is "A refusal to grant the truth of something."

People deny for many reasons—and I believe people should think critically about something like STYLE Technology and not just accept something as important as STYLE on face value. But some people deny because they don't think—or because they are afraid to think deeply—about themselves—and others.

People may deny because they are surprised that the STYLE concept exists and need more time to work it out. They may deny because they don't like looking at themselves and see potential criticism of their behavior (even though the point is made again and again there is no wrong STYLE). Some may deny because basic STYLE concept is so simple and their belief is that something this powerful can't be simple.

People who understand STYLE quickly, and witness others in denial, comment on the behavior they see. Let's call the person witnessing as the *Observer*, and the person denying as the *Denier*. The Denier uses behavior while denying which is like their STYLE. This is so very obvious to the Observer, that the Observer's belief in the concept is proven by witnessing the Denier. **What the Observer sees is:**

- **Denying Analyticals**—deep in contemplation, will postpone their decision of accepting STYLE and ask numerous questions to gather data.
- **Denying Drivers**—will engage in semi-aggressive parry and thrust sometimes becoming autocratic by competitively throwing half considered facts at the instructor to address.
- **Denying Amiables**—not wanting to upset the instructor, will stay very quiet and when asked if they have questions, will timidly ask questions which are not always questions, but statements of doubt.
- **Denying Expressives**—thinking out loud, sometimes talk themselves into, and then out of, several points as they carry on a conversation with themselves.

Most of us go through some form of denial. Some stay there longer than others. Most eventually accept that there is truth in STYLE. Let me take the big risk here, and tell it like the Expressive I am.

We all have STYLE!

There, I stuck my neck out and took a firm stand on the issue.

Chapter Five

THE ANALYTICAL

"The Need To Be Correct"

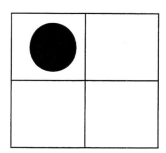

> **WARNING**
> This chapter presents a collection of behaviors and comforts about each STYLE and is designed to indicate positive Differences, not to label a STYLE with right or wrong behavior. It is important to recognize that this is a generic attempt to understand *some* of the components of the STYLE, not the person.

CLUE FINDING

OBSERVING

Watch for formal and controlled body language; facial expressions that seldom change; and with very controlled reactive Analyticals little or no emotion. The Analytical may have little eye contact, looking instead at papers and objects. They may display indifference and unconcern. They may be slow to act.

LISTENING

You might hear little tonal change, slow word pace as if...at times...they were...selecting...each word, and being cautious. Usually, they do not talk in terms of feelings or beliefs...and will instead substitute facts, numbers, or principles. They will tend to avoid making direct statements and decisions.

STRENGTHS

Exacting	Methodical
Thorough	Industrious
Steady	Orderly
Cautious	Punctual
Conscientious	Factual
Deliberating	Detail oriented

LIABILITIES   In addition to doing any or all the above in extreme, the Analytical may avoid risks and gather data without reaching a conclusion. This can cause productivity to be put on hold, a project to never be completed, or progress to stop. Doing this, the Analytical may personally be missing some opportunities in life.

The Analytical needs someone to give them information, facts, time, and then low-key persuasion through questioning in order to decide.

It is best if emotions are not used as an appeal.

NEED   The Analytical has a strong need to be right and be seen as an expert, or very knowledgeable.

This is illustrated in the Analytical's actions to have detailed information, to use a lengthy decision making process, and to avoid being rushed into commitment.

SURPRISES   (How an Analytical may do things differently than their STYLE suggests.)

An Analytical may at times make what seem to be quick actions or decisions. This may be due to the Analytical having obtained enough data, and has reached a decision on the right choice or action. You are just observing the end of the process.

An Analytical may also become very opinionated, taking a firm stand on something. This may be due to having studied the task and having reached a "right" decision due to the careful research process.

This person needs new facts to change his or her mind.

The more *Flexibility* the Analytical has and uses, the more he or she will seem to do things unlike their STYLE.

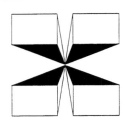

How Do We
Get Them To Respond?

Analyticals respond more favorably when we allow them to use their process of engineering the decision. They will appreciate (although not usually show it) our patience in supplying the information they need and the time to analyze it.

If we are more Tell Assertive and rush the decision, or if we are a more Emote Reactive STYLE and show discomfort with their seemingly less responsive behavior, we run the risk of them not cooperating with us.

STYLEBYTE

Like all other STYLES there are many different types of Analyticals. Some have qualities of other STYLES and there will be behaviors demonstrated unlike what this book says an Analytical should be.

All Analyticals will have a predominance of the behaviors and comforts stated in this chapter—after all, that is what makes them Analyticals.

In my work I have associates and friends who are Analytical. Some dress flamboyantly, or are entertainers, others are very outgoing and charming, or have a tremendous sense of humor. They may display other characteristics one might be surprised about because we always expect the Analytical to be serious and conservative.

All of the people I mentioned have most of the book characteristics as well, and that is the point. Those things that make one a certain STYLE are there, but so are many other facets and qualities which make up our uniqueness as human beings.

Chapter Six

THE DRIVER

"The Need For Control"

> **WARNING**
> This chapter presents a collection of behaviors and comforts about each STYLE and is designed to indicate positive Differences, not to label a STYLE with right or wrong behavior. It is important to recognize that this is a generic attempt to understand *some* of the components of the STYLE, not the person.

CLUE FINDING

OBSERVING   Watch for controlled body language and direct eye contact. Drivers may get impatient and will risk to get what they want—right now. They will be on task and seem in a hurry. Drivers may be fast to act.

LISTENING   The Driver's tone may be powerful, but even. Their voice can be forceful, and they may even interrupt others. Drivers talk about immediate time frames and are not seemingly concerned about the past or future. They use time efficiently.

STRENGTHS

Direct	Disciplined
Objective	Task Oriented
Decisive	Demanding
Practical	Tough
Efficient	Independent thinker

Pioneering   Strong-willed
Risk taker   Forceful

LIABILITIES   In addition to doing any or all the above in extreme, the Driver may act so fast on the task that
personal relationships may be ignored. This will
alienate others and cause some people to compete
in the future because of the revenge factor.

The Driver needs someone to supply bottom line
facts and then let the Driver choose from options.
This person should not react to what may seem to
be the lack of caring from the Driver.

NEED   The Driver has a strong need for control or power.
The Driver displays this by their need to control
their emotions, controlling the decision making
process, or changing the rules from time to time.

SURPRISES   (How a Driver may do things differently than their
STYLE suggests.)

The Driver may display a high degree of personal
concern, and even affection at times. Many times
this is due to the task having been completed or
nearly completed. It also may be due to the fact
that Drivers have as many feelings as anyone else
and they see the personal issue as a priority.

The Driver may need someone to listen and give
recognition to their thinking or concern and then
go back to the task. **The more *Flexibility* the
Driver has and uses, the more he or she will
seem to do things unlike their STYLE.**

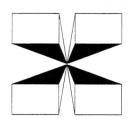

How Do We Get Them To Respond?

Working with a Driver is fast paced and we must be ready to tell or ask when the Driver is ready. Giving the "bottom line" is an overused expression, but one that aptly fits in getting a Driver to respond. If you are Ask Assertive, this means speeding up your way of doing things.

Staying on task may look uncaring at times to those who are Emote Reactive, but if they do not take this behavior personally, they stand a better chance of getting their needs met.

STYLEBYTE

One of the most feeling people I have known is a Driver. She demonstrates most of the outward behaviors the Driver is supposed to have—those of *Control*—being on task, formal, factual, business like—and those of *Tell*—being fast moving, a quick decision maker, directing others.

At the same time, when she lets someone inside to know the person beneath the STYLE there is this incredible depth of feeling and emotion not at all apparent on the surface.

If you are Emote, it is difficult to see this real person at times.

If you are not a Driver, it is important to know that you can hurt a Driver's feelings. So, being polite and diplomatic still counts.

It is important to know that this person can have a strong intuitive sense driven by feelings. This sense can fuel their creativity and make them as sensitive as anyone.

You may not see these qualities—but they are there.

Remember these things about the Drivers in your life and let this knowledge give those relationships more meaning and understanding.

Chapter Seven

THE AMIABLE

"The Need For Support"

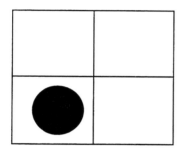

WARNING	

WARNING
This chapter presents a collection of behaviors and comforts about each STYLE and is designed to indicate positive Differences, not to label a STYLE with right or wrong behavior. It is important to recognize that this is a generic attempt to understand *some* of the components of the STYLE, not the person.

CLUE FINDING

OBSERVING

Watch for relaxed posture that displays openness and emotion. They may sit back and their gestures will not be threatening. Eye contact may not be strong if there is personal tension, otherwise eye contact will be checking for support. They may show through body language a need for reassurance and encouragement. Amiables may be slow to act.

STRENGTHS

Agreeable	Friendly
Conventional	Compliant
Helpful	Tolerant
Patient	Likable
People Oriented	Sensitive
Easy Going	Pliable

LIABILITIES

In addition to doing any or all the above in extreme, the Amiable may say "yes" to protect the relationship and then have to *back out* of the commitment later. This may be due to not enough time to complete it, or an unwillingness to comply because of safety or value conflict. This can be frustrating in relationships, and cause the Amiable to be perceived as weak...which may not be the case.

The Amiable needs someone to check with them more than once...being careful not to force them into making too fast a decision. This is best accomplished by checking on how they *feel* about things, and then supporting them to a safe decision.

NEED

The Amiable has a strong need to be interpersonally secure and free from criticism.

The Amiable shows this through taking the necessary time to protect the relationship, by not deciding until he or she feels safe, and by looking at decisions from the point of view of the people involved.

SURPRISES   (How an Amiable may do things differently than their STYLE suggests.)

An Amiable may become tenacious about a given position. Once they have reached a decision on what they feel is the *safe* decision concerning themselves, or others, they will stand firm and need careful support (not only facts!) to change their mind.

One example is the Amiable manager who believes that a certain policy will negatively affect his employees. He might become very *Tell* in defending his stand against the policy because he believes it is safer to modify his behavior than see his employees hurt.

Someone working to change the Amiable's opinion would need to be patient and listen. Then, by giving evidence that shows how the policy supports the manager's employees (and not just facts about the productivity of the decision) will the Amiable consider changing his mind.

The more *Flexibility* the Amiable has and uses, the more he or she will seem to do things unlike their STYLE.

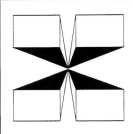

How Do We
Get Them To Respond?

If you are more Tell Assertive, you may think the Amiable is cooperating with you and in agreement. You could be very wrong. To motivate the Amiable you must have patience and draw them out by asking questions and listening to them. Then you will have earned your right to present what it is you want.

If you are Control Reactive, you must support the Amiable's need to express feelings and work out the people side of things. Being patient here and contributing to this thought process by making suggestions is key in gaining cooperation.

STYLEBYTE

Those who are Amiable can be very strong people. This is another one of those characteristics that are not always apparent when we observe just the STYLE.

I have seen Amiables face tragedy and be the pillar of strength the entire family clings to. I have seen Amiables successful in tough business situations and rock hard in difficult stress ridden jobs.

If you are not Amiable, you might not realize just how capable this person can be. You might question if this nice, quiet, friendly person has got what it takes.

You might be very wrong in this belief.

When the Amiable *becomes determined and personally motivated*, like people of all STYLES, they have incredible drive and energy. And because of this personal motivation, what they don't know—they will learn; and what they can't do—they will find a way of doing.

Remember these things with Amiables in your life. Don't sell them short.

Chapter Eight

THE EXPRESSIVE

"The Need For Recognition"

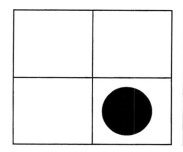

> **WARNING**
> This chapter presents a collection of behaviors and comforts about each STYLE and is designed to indicate positive Differences, not to label a STYLE with right or wrong behavior. It is important to recognize that this is a generic attempt to understand *some* of the components of the STYLE, not the person.

CLUE FINDING

OBSERVING

Watch for the changing facial expressions and body language that moves frequently. Eye contact may be strong, and take in everyone, often sweeping the room. Expressives may be fast to act.

LISTENING

Tone fluctuates and varies. They are excitable, motivating...even dramatic!...in their emphasis and pace. They may talk through the start of other appointments, so time gets away...but they usually are in a hurry to move to something they want.

STRENGTHS

Enthusiastic	Quick
Adaptable	Generous
Spontaneous	Resourceful
Optimistic	Charming
Creative	Open
Dramatic	Action oriented

LIABILITIES

In addition to doing any or all of the above in extreme, the Expressive may become more emotional about a given set of circumstances than others may feel is necessary. This behavior may cause the Expressive to harm his or her relationships and alienate co-workers, customers, managers, or significant others.

The Expressive needs someone to have patience, listen, and not react to emotional outbursts. Many times the Expressive feels genuine remorse for having had a potentially destructive outburst. At this time, a helpful person needs to offer more logical suggestions after the Expressive has calmed down.

NEED

The Expressive has a strong need for recognition and visibility.

Expressives show this by body language, voice and words which may be dramatic and call attention, taking social risks, making decisions that put them in the *limelight*

SURRIPRISES   (How an Expressive may do things differently than their STYLE suggests.)

The Expressive may become very intent on gathering data, and taking time to make a decision. This may be due to enjoying the process of looking and not necessarily due to finding the *right* decision. The Expressive may need someone to listen to what he or she is discovering and then encourage a decision.

The more *Flexibility* the Expressive has and uses, the more he or she will seem to do things unlike their STYLE.

How Do We Get Them To Respond?

Getting the Expressive to respond involves listening to them and letting them run with what they are thinking. Then, get them to task by Asking about relevant issues. If you are Tell Assertive, it means you must give up *some* of your need to Tell.

Of you are Control Reactive, remember the feelings and ideas that may flow so quickly from the Expressive are a means for this person to *think out loud* and allowing that process will earn your right to move to your needs.

STYLEBYTE

OK, you know I'm an Expressive, so you figure I have a lot to say about this STYLE. Well, I'll try real hard to keep this STYLEBYTE the same size as the others.

Expressives can have depth and strength and goodness just as people of all STYLES can have those things.

Sometimes Expressives attract the misunderstanding that they can't stick to details, or finish something they start, or can't stay on task.

There are Expressives who have difficulty with those things, but again I will invoke the power of personal motivation and make this point for Expressives and all STYLES.

The more an Expressive (or any person of any other STYLE) is personally motivated to accomplish something, the more they will focus energy to do it. This can help them be on task, pay attention to details, and finish what they start.

Now, I have measured the other three STYLEBYTES in this series and determined Analytically that this one takes no more space than the others.

For the most part.

Kinda.

Chapter Nine

DETERMINING YOUR OWN STYLE

"We All Have STYLE"

The best way to arrive at your own STYLE is to be profiled by others using a profiling instrument. These instruments many times are computer scored, very accurate, and you can obtain one through the publisher.

For our purposes here, determining your own STYLE is not as difficult as it might seem at first. The first thing to be aware of is you probably have a place which is most comfortable for you to be on the map (your normal home). Next, this place is a position intersecting on the Assertiveness line and on the Reactiveness line. Don't get hung up on the fact that you can be all over, or that you are all over the map—you probably can be, but don't let that bother you for now.

DETERMINING ASSERTIVENESS

TELL

Your Assertiveness is an aspect of how you attempt to get your way with others. Think about your behavior when dealing with others about things important to you. How you communicate what you want. Are you direct, meaning do you make statements like *"Let's do this..."* or *"Try this..."*. These are *telling statements*, and even if the words expressed in them are not your words, the purpose of the statement is to *tell* the other person what it is you want. You're not asking them.

How about your decision making? Have others told you to slow down? Do you seem to arrive at what to do before others? Do some think you a risk taker, or someone who *pioneers* the way? Are you the one who *gets others going*? It is important to know the questions just asked are about you in general, not about you with one person, but with more than one in many aspects of your life.

If these questions are generally true about you, or more true than the Ask Assertive questions which follow, place a dot somewhere to the right of center on the Assertiveness Graph on page 63.

ASK

Are you generally comfortable waiting for others to decide first? Are you concerned if you say things too quickly others may get the wrong idea, or that it may be impolite, or inaccurate? Does this cause you to hesitate to make a commitment at times even when you have made up your mind? Do you more frequently ask questions like *"Have you tried this...?"* or *"I wonder what would happen if...?"*. Are you trying to suggest that course of action, but may not want to come right out and advocate it? Do others tell you to move quicker, or to get ready or prepared faster?

These are examples of *asking statements* and even if the words are not yours, the purpose behind them is to suggest actions rather than command them. You may greatly want others to do what you suggest, but you do not want to tell them to do it.

If these questions are generally true or more true than the **Tell Assertive** questions, place a dot somewhere to the left of center on the Assertiveness Graph.

ASSERTIVENESS GRAPH

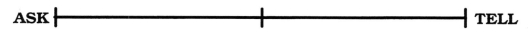

ASK |—————————————————+—————————————————| **TELL**

You should now have only one dot on this chart. It should be to the right of center if you feel you are more Tell Assertive, or to the left of center if you feel you are more Ask Assertive.

DETERMINING REACTIVENESS

CONTROL

Do you hold your feelings in check? Is it uncomfortable for you to be outwardly emotional? Would you rather the conversation stays on the point, and doesn't go aside to how the other person feels about it? Do you find yourself wanting others not to be *so emotional about it?*

When making decisions do you find yourself gathering the facts, and not using your *gut* reaction until later? At social gatherings do you find yourself being factual and calmer in discussions than some of the others? Are you prone to be a *bit more formal?* When upset with someone, do you not show your feelings and remain unemotional? Have you been told to smile more, or that you look like you don't care?

If these questions are generally true, or more true than the questions about **Emote** which follow, place a dot above center on the Reactiveness Graph on page 64.

EMOTE

Are you free with your emotions? Do they, at times, *just come out?* When you talk with others, are you sharing feelings—concerns, wishes, wants, or opinions? When you have a good day, or a bad one, do you let others know? Do you like to smile and / or go through facial changes when you speak?

Do you consider yourself *approachable*? Do you encourage others to *let it out* and talk about *how they feel?* Have others asked you not to be *so emotional*, or said you should *stay in control more?* In social situations are you prone to *let it out* emotionally? Do you feel it is important to *socialize* or to *get to know someone personally?*

If these questions are generally true, or more true than the questions about **Control**, place a dot below center on the Reactiveness Graph.

CONTROL

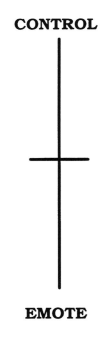

EMOTE

REACTIVENESS GRAPH

MERGING THE POSITIONS

When overlaying the Assertive Graph (with your dot) and the Reactive Graph (with your dot), you have determined a major STYLE quadrant at the point where the dots would intersect. The map below suggests a fictional intersection.

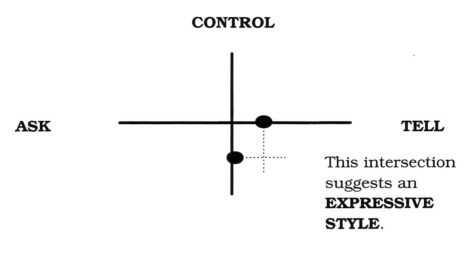

This intersection suggests an **EXPRESSIVE STYLE**.

On the following Map, indicate the position where your dots would intersect.

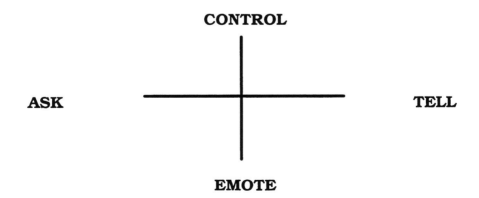

IN ADDITION

Profiling tools are available which have different selection criteria. Two broad ways to look at these tools is *how they are administered.* They can be:

As *you* see you—which is **self scored.**

As *others* see you—which is **surveyed by others.**

By far, the profile that shows you how others see you, as well as giving you feedback on how others see your Flexibility, is the more valuable method.

Why?

We are not always accurate when we fill out an instrument about ourselves. It is difficult to be self-critical, and we humans have a tendency to bias these kinds of instruments.

THE COMPUTER PROFILE

There are computer instruments available which help you to determine your STYLE, or will show something similar to STYLE.

The advantage here is the honesty and accuracy of the feedback.

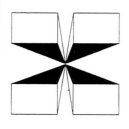

How Do We
Get Them To Respond?

Our own STYLE influences others in how they respond to us. If we display behavior which is comfortable to others, we stand a greater chance to motivate the other person to want to work with us.

If our goal is the response of others to some need we have, then it is best to let others be their STYLE and for us to not insist that our STYLE comforts get met. That means temporarily holding back our Assertiveness or Reactiveness until the other person has used theirs. Staying more in the middle of the STYLE map for a little while rather than promoting our corner of it will earn greater response.

STYLEBYTE

There is an excellent tool—The **INTERPERSONAL STYLE INDICATOR**, designed by Ralph Colby—which helps determine your **STYLE** and **Flexibility**. In it, you select five people important to you to complete a survey. The survey results are entered into computer software and reports based on the information are generated. This tool can be very helpful to you and is very effective because it indicates how others see your STYLE.

One significant advantage of such a profile instrument, which enlists the feedback of others, is that the participant learns how others might react to their STYLE. They can better determine how to make interactions positive experiences. Relationships can be affected—improving trust, communication, cooperation, and ultimately influencing the other person's decision making.

Information about how to order The INTERPERSONAL STYLE INDICATOR is on page 123.

Chapter Ten

DETERMINING THE STYLE OF OTHERS

"Watch, Listen, Think—Then Decide"

To determine **STYLE** it is important to look for several behaviors. The trap is to say, *"This person is fact oriented, therefore he must be Analytical."* This decision could be incorrect if the person turns out to be a Driver, who is also fact oriented .

An Expressive could be fact oriented because of the importance of the decision and therefore appear to have some Analytical tendencies at the moment.

THREE MAJOR WAYS TO DETERMINE STYLE

- **Observation** (including listening)

- **Questioning** (including direct and indirect questioning)

- **History** (including primary and secondary information)

OBSERVATION
Observation is by far the fastest method to determine STYLE, and can also be quite accurate if applied correctly.

OBSERVE and listen to:

- **Facial expressions/hand movements/quickness or slowness of movement**
- **Tone of voice / pace of speech / quality of speech (harsh, warmth, inflection, etc.)**
- **Thoughts and thinking process as verbalized (values, beliefs, ideas, etc.)**

Remember, the absence of BODY LANGUAGE...*is* body language.

QUESTIONING

Questioning can be a skill employed both directly and indirectly as a way of determining STYLE. It is combined with seeing and listening for best results.

DIRECT QUESTIONING includes questions you ask for the sole purpose of determining STYLE. It may not always be necessary to use direct questions, as the STYLE may be readily definable through the other methods. When it isn't, try questions like:

- **How would you prefer we work together?**

- **What do you expect of me in working with this (task, project, relationship, etc.)?**

- **What decision making process is most comfortable for you?**

The answers to these types of questions can give insight to someone's STYLE by how they are answered. For example:

An Amiable or Expressive may stress relationship-oriented answers, such as *"by working closely together"* or *"contact me any time."*

A Driver or an Analytical may answer by describing more independent reactions, such as *"call me only under _____ situations"* or *"I'll call you."*

(When using these methods, observe body language and listen to the person's voice.)

The preceding are only two examples of direct questioning. Use your imagination based on what you know about the comforts of STYLE and you will find unlimited combinations of direct questions.

Your questions should not be too personal in nature, especially if you expect the person is a Driver or an Analytical.

Try INDIRECT QUESTIONING when direct questions are too personal, or inappropriate. This method is simply asking the questions you would routinely ask in connection with the normal course of your work. Then, through observing the responses (body language, tone, pace, word selection, etc.), you can determine STYLE.

Many times, indirect questions are all that need to be asked. If you are experiencing difficulty determining STYLE, then go to the direct method, taking care to be diplomatic.

Determining STYLE is important. So, if indirect methods don't give you enough data, take the *risk* to be more direct. The risk indicated here is interpersonal. It is minimal as long as the direct method is not used excessively.

HISTORY

History is a study of data which you may have about the person. History is gathered in two ways:

Secondary—which is information someone gives you about the person, or you have from correspondence or telephone contact; or...

Primary—which is a study of information resulting from a meeting with the person.

Obtain SECONDARY INFORMATION by asking questions of those familiar with the person whose STYLE you are attempting to determine. Some examples:

■ *"How fast does this person make decisions?"*

■ *"Is she mostly businesslike?"* or *"Does she like to talk about non-business matters?"*

Once again, use your imagination from what you know about STYLE comforts to find numerous questions. Make sure you ask more than one question, and often it is helpful to ask the question more than one way. If the person you are asking does not understand STYLE Technology they may have a conflicting definition to *businesslike* or *task oriented*—you may need to repeat the question in a slightly different way.

When using the telephone use listening clues, or when reading, use word clues based on what you know about STYLE comforts.

Confirm PRIMARY INFORMATION by simply checking what you observed...or asked...against what you know about STYLE comforts and then arriving at a conclusion about the STYLE.

Whatever method you use, be prepared to change your mind from the initial observation if stronger evidence comes forth. Allowing yourself to change your mind will contribute greatly to recognizing the real STYLE.

QUICK PROFILING

We tend to *get* one or the other of the dimensions—either Assertiveness or Reactiveness first because most everyone demonstrates more prominent aspects of one or the other dimension readily.

Ask yourself if you see the person to be *above or below the line* (meaning Control or Emote). Then ask yourself is he *to the right or the left* (meaning Tell or Ask). Work out the STYLE in this manner and you will be less likely to make errors.

Once you have determined the major STYLE quadrant, you can then ask the same questions *inside* that quadrant. In this manner, you can actually determine the *sub-quadrant* as outlined in Chapter Four.

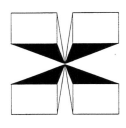

How Do We
Get Them To Respond?

In using any of the Determining STYLE methods in the previous material, make your decisions based on asking, "How Tell or Ask Assertive is this person?" and "How Emote or Control Reactive is this person?"

By doing this and adding up the behavior clues like a detective, you will arrive at a much more accurate decision about a person's STYLE. You can then take the appropriate actions to earn desired responses such as improved trust, communication, cooperation, and decision making.

STYLEBYTE

DON'T SUFFER FROM DART THROWING!!!!

Dart Throwing

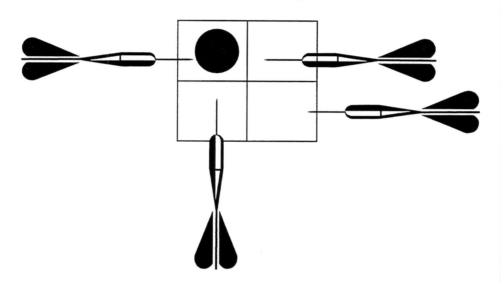

Dart Throwing is taking one or two quick clues in isolation and saying something like, *"Since this person asks questions, they must be an Analytical."* This will fool you; it's like throwing darts at the STYLE Map.

Work out the STYLE dimensionally by asking yourself *"how assertive"* and then *"how reactive"* is the person.

Chapter Eleven

INFLUENCING WITH STYLE

"Flexibility Is What Counts"

The next several chapters deal with the most important aspects of the book—**Application**. We will discuss effective skills for use in working with each STYLE to accomplish various interpersonal goals including:

- reduce personal tension
- build trust
- seek cooperation
- find more business
- manage more effectively
- enjoy better relationships

AWARENESS OF THE COMFORT ZONE OR STYLE OF THE OTHER PERSON

There are several factors which add to developing more positive STYLE relationships. Everyone is unique. We all have certain preferences that can be obvious in our behavior. By recognizing this behavior, we have clues to how others like to be treated. For example, ...

An Amiable or Expressive person may demonstrate their preferences by their openness, warmth, or friendliness. This person may want to talk about personal matters, or just make small talk.

The Driver or Analytical person may, on the other hand, be poker faced, non-emotional, and slightly distant or aloof. This person may be most comfortable if we get down to business quickly and not make small talk.

AWARENESS OF YOUR STYLE

Your own unique preferences influence your comfort. These can get in the way of your relationships with others.

For example, you may be Analytical and very concerned with details. Working with others who don't get the facts can be irritating to you when you see details as important to the successful completion of a job or any task.

If your Expressive associate doesn't listen to the details that may be important to their success with your project, you may be frustrated with their level of comfort.

This will be even more frustrating if they complain later about something, when you may feel they should have listened.

AWARENESS OF HOW YOUR STYLE AFFECTS OTHERS

Our preferences, which are right for us, may be uncomfortable, irritating, or even unpleasant to others. How your comfort preferences may influence the comfort positively or negatively of others is something of which to be knowledgeable.

For example, as an Analytical, your same attention to details may cause others discomfort, because they may want to socialize instead of getting down to business.

The Amiable or Expressive employee who likes to chat may be uncomfortable if you don't spend some time socializing. Too much task can be negative to this person's comfort and productivity.

In other words, this person works better...with higher quality...if they can **Emote**, than if they had to keep to the task at all times.

FLEXIBILITY

Flexibility, sometimes called **Versatility**, is the most important aspect of working with STYLE. It is also one of the most important aspects of the success of interpersonal or group relationships.

> **FLEXIBILITY can be defined as the amount of effort, or observable energy, a person expends in meeting the interpersonal needs of others.**

In other words, how comfortable others are in the way we treat them based upon their STYLE, not ours.

> **If there is a GOLDEN RULE OF STYLE, the major point to be made about working with STYLE is to:**
>
> *"Treat Others The Way They Wish To Be Treated, Not What Is Comfortable For You."*

SELF MANAGEMENT

An important aspect of Flexibility is personal **Self Management**.

SELF MANAGEMENT is being aware of Flexibility and choosing to use it.

If one **chooses to be Flexible**, that means a Self Management choice has been made also. Self Management may mean:

■ Having patience with STYLES slower or faster to act than you, or patience if the other person deals with facts or feelings and this is not your comfort.

■ Understanding if the other person is concerned with the risk of telling you what they are feeling or thinking, and thus are not communicating. Patience on your part comes into play here. Being patient and *self managing* while you—a Driver, draw out the other person—an Amiable concerned with this risk.

■ Not reacting in kind to emotional outbursts, personal attack, indecision, autocratic behavior, attempts to avoid—or if the other person is off on any STYLE-related tangent...(being emotional or objective).

■ Being aware that some behaviors displayed and words used by others do not necessarily represent the real concern or problem that others have. Self management means staying with the person until you have the real issue surfaced. Again, this takes patience.

FLEXIBILITY MAPPING

The following Flexibility Map gives a basic idea of how to be flexible with each STYLE.

There are many other factors involved in Flexibility, and many are situational—requiring doing the right thing at the right time. The best skills for this are listening and observing. Being patient—using Self Management, and applying this knowledge—will be very effective in influencing STYLE.

ANALYTICAL **(help them be right)** Demonstrate through actions how you can be helpful, give written detail, take time and support thinking process, don't over-sell or over state, do what you say you will do. Listen to them and be patient when they ask for more detail.	**DRIVER** **(help them remain in control)** Don't waste time, get down to business, supply facts not opinions. Provide options for them to make decisions, don't be too quick to form a personal relationship. Give brief, factual answers to their questions.
AMIABLE **(help them be secure)** Show interest in the person, take time to develop a personal relationship, draw them out and listen patiently while not interrupting. Don't rush the decision or try to decide for them.	**EXPRESSIVE** **(help them be recognized)** Be energetic and listen to their ideas, opinions, and dreams. Give feelings, testimonials, and incentives. Work on building personal relationships, don't argue—listen. Be stimulating and keep a high energy level apparent.

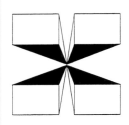

How Do We
Get Them To Respond?

Flexibility is what most of these How Do We Get Them To Respond? summary segments have been all about. If you go back over them, you will find a basic primer on Flexibility which is really how you get others to respond.

Using Flexibility is investing something. It is an investment of energy with the dividend of positive response as the return. The response could mean people work harder, or better, or a customer buys, or a significant other sees your need and helps support it.

If the potential response (or another way of saying it— the *people objective*) is important enough, then *the investment is worth the effort.*

STYLEBYTE

There is no stronger point to make about STYLE than Flexibility. It is the reason we study STYLE. It is the factor which separates this technology from all the-nice-to-know stuff. There is a tremendous difference between *knowing* and *doing*. Without doing something to improve our Flexibility, we sit in the spectator seat of life—never getting into the game. The game is played without us and we lose if we stay in that seat.

The point that Flexibility is a *skill* and a *choice* must also be emphasized. We all have some Flexibility skill and great potential for skill, but many times we choose not to use it or fulfill our potential.

There are some simple rules for growing your ability to be Flexible. Like any other skill—the more you use it and grow it—the more comfortable and easy it becomes. Here are some *bottom line* growth points:

**Amiables can become more Flexible...
if they would "Tell" more.
Analyticals can become more Flexible...
if they would "Decide" more.
Drivers can become more Flexible...
if they would "Ask" more.
Expressives can become more Flexible...
if they would "Listen" more.**

These ideas are not all that hard to understand, and *so simple*...so simple, but not necessarily easy.

Chapter Twelve

DIFFICULT PEOPLE—
DIFFICULT SITUATIONS

"People Need Help At A Time Like This"

Most people who present you with difficult situations are not difficult people. Their tension is high due to some stress factor, or factors. This gets in the way of accomplishing outcomes in our career and personal life. Since STYLE plays a surprising part in working with many of these situations—this chapter will look at what is happening and what to do to accomplish the outcome you want.

FIGHT AND FLIGHT

When stress becomes intense, each interpersonal STYLE may react in behavior patterns comfortable to them. These patterns are observed through the classic defensive behaviors—**fight** and **flight**.

FIGHT may be seen when a person ...confronts, demands, or attacks.

FLIGHT may be observed when a person...avoids, leaves, stalls, or cannot be contacted.

Witnessing this behavior does not necessarily mean defensiveness is involved, but should be a red flag that stress is high.

In the illustration below, we see how fight may be an initial choice of Tell Assertive STYLES, whereas flight may be a first choice of Ask Assertives.

DEFENSIVE BEHAVIOR BY STYLE

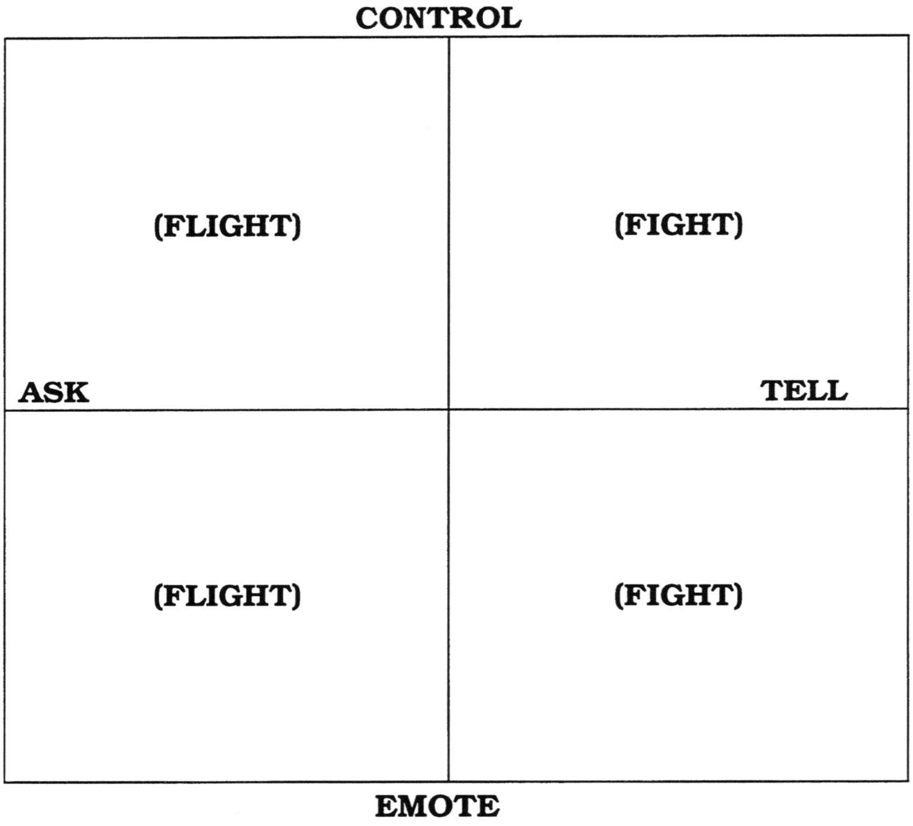

CONTROL

(FLIGHT)	**(FIGHT)**
ASK	**TELL**
(FLIGHT)	**(FIGHT)**

EMOTE

This is logical since Tell Assertives are more naturally comfortable confronting, and Ask Assertives more comfortable avoiding direct confrontation.

Each STYLE has a unique behavior set in how they display defensive behavior. Sometimes called back-up STYLE, this behavior is outlined below.

STYLE DEFENSIVE BEHAVIOR

CONTROL

(AVOID)	**(DEMAND)**
ASK	**TELL**
(GIVE-IN)	**(ATTACK)**

EMOTE

STYLE DEFENSIVE BEHAVIOR

Each of these defensive states are destructive to relationships and are not productive. When you find yourself in a discussion with a customer, a team member, coworker, employee, supervisor, or significant other who seems defensive, they may be influenced at that moment by stress, threat, or fear of some kind.

The stress or underlying fear which causes the defensiveness MUST be reduced before anything productive can be accomplished with this person.

If this is getting in the way of something you wish to accomplish and you want to affect a positive outcome, there are skills to work on with defensive STYLE behavior.

Understanding that emotion can play a major part in Style Defensive Behavior is an important step in helping clear up the situation.

It isn't the other person's EMOTION that is the most dangerous at these times...it is yours. Your SELF MANAGEMENT and FLEXIBILITY are very important, and your emotion can get in the way of using them effectively

---

This is a time when your calmness and skill can be most beneficial. Whenever you are confronted with defensiveness, remain absolutely calm, and listen to what the person is saying without reaction.

LSQPA—A SKILL SET TO DEAL WITH DEFENSIVE BEHAVIOR

To lower tension and change perception, we can use the skills of **LSQPA**. It is **a natural process, not a set of tricky phrases. It can be very powerful, particularly as you become more skillful at using it with STYLE defensive behavior or many other** *difficult* **interpersonal situations.**

LSQPA is ...

> **L—isten**
>
> **S—hare**
>
> **Q—uestion**
>
> **P—resent**
>
> **A—sk**

LISTEN

> **L = Listen to the concern without judgment, defensiveness, or ridicule.**

The only talking you should do at this point is to ask questions like:

"Tell me more about that."
"Could you give me an example?"

Do not give in to the temptation to present anything at this time—just be supportive.

SHARE

S = Share the person's feelings.

Don't agree with the concern, just the person's right to display the concern. Sharing might be just repeating what the person has said to confirm you heard. Sharing is also using empathy statements like:

> *"I see your concern."*
> *"Your concern is not unusual."*
> *"I would be wondering that too."*

By using these expressions, you are establishing commonality—not agreeing that the fear is real—just acknowledging their right to have it. Your attitude is one that says, *"I understand you are apprehensive, even though it's unnecessary."* or *"I might think that, too."*

You still are not trying to defend, answer, or argue—you are just staying on the same side as the other person.

QUESTION

Q = Question to obtain clarification; find out the real issues.

Don't just believe what the person is saying on the surface. These questions should dig deeply, to get at the hidden agenda, or the real concern, and get it out in the open. This may sound like, *"I hear what you're saying, also I would be concerned whether I was going to be treated fairly. Has fairness crossed your mind?"* (Or, some question appropriate to the situation.)

The idea is to get the person to talk about the fear, or what is causing the stress. Talking about these things can calm the person.

This is extremely important, as the only way you can hope to help the person overcome their fear (and help affect your desired outcome) is to get it out in the open where it *can be shown to not be a real factor.* Most fears won't happen, unless the person doesn't do anything to prevent them.

NOTE
This Listening—Sharing—Questioning cycle can be effective with all STYLES. Stay with these skills, repeating them as necessary, until tension has been reduced. When the person is more relaxed, and is cooperating, or participating more with you move on.

PRESENT

P = Present evidence to neutralize,...and reduce the fear.

Give help and assistance in whatever way is needed to solve this emotional problem for the person. This may be presenting testimonials of others who are successful doing what you suggest. It may also be showing how you will help, or share the risk.

The STYLE influencing map in Chapter Eleven suggests ways to *present* to each STYLE.

ASK

> **A = Ask for agreement.**

Basically, this is where you close the transaction. Here you obtain commitment or get approval to go ahead, implement, or take the next logical step.

If the tension hasn't gone down, go through the process again, and find what else is getting in the way.

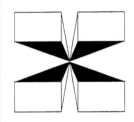

How Do We Get Them To Respond?

LSQPA is a natural process.

Using this process motivates others. Remember our objectives—to build skill in influencing:

**TRUST
COMMUNICATION
COOPERATION
DECISION MAKING**

LSQPA can be used when there is a lack of response in any of the objectives.

STYLEBYTE

LSQPA

I can't think of any other thing I can give you (or actually pass on to you as I didn't invent it) than **LSQPA**.

LSQPA, and processes like it, are the epitome of *Knowing* and *Doing*. It is one of the most powerful skill sets which facilitates Flexibility.

It is a gift.

And it is a gift to be used—not paraded out for some special event or kept locked in the display case of life. It should be used any time there is tension, or resistance, or you are communicating with someone who is angry, or worried.

Sometimes things we find difficult to do are indications we need to grow in some area. We can't improve or be effective with others by just doing that which is comfortable.

Different STYLES will find different parts of LSQPA comfortable and difficult.

Drivers and Expressives will have natural skills at *Presenting* and want to go there when confronted with life's challenges.

Drivers and Expressives must practice the Flexibility skills of *Listening—really Listening—*and take the time to be effective at *Questioning.* Driver and Expressive people will become impressive and strong interpersonally using this process if they would work in these areas.

Amiables and Analyticals will need to eventually leave their beloved listening and questioning to *Present* with conviction after they have used their natural strengths.

People of these two STYLES will be dynamic and persuasive with this process if they would learn to be more comfortable *Presenting.*

All STYLES must use the empathy of *Sharing,* and the accountability of *Asking* to complete their mastery.

The prospect of mastery level interpersonal communication can be reached with the effective use of this process. This level does not need to be reached; however, for the benefits of using LSQPA to start pouring into one's life.

Imagine how much more effective and successful one can become using LSQPA to manage the opportunities which present themselves daily. The process helps you get through your daily life events and each time you use it you automatically enhance and grow your success potential with others.

Chapter Thirteen

HOW NOT TO BE CONTROLLED BY STYLE

"This One's Up To You!"

We as human beings can be influenced by others. This is not bad or negative in itself, as we need to have an open mind in considering the possibilities in life, and the council and opinions of others is a major source of information. Sometimes we are influenced for the better.

Sometimes we may be unduly influenced by others, and must guard against those who have negative intent, or are incompetent to advise or even report on something. This is life—a constant sorting out of information and impressions broadcast by the media and those around us.

> **Sometimes the STYLE of others alone can influence us. This is inappropriate because we are then reacting to behavior, comfort, and habits—not values, morals, intelligence, insight, education, wisdom, and experience**.

Imagine the situation where your Expressive teenager is turned on by the Expressive friend who, through warmth and enthusiasm takes him or her to the wrong party, and at the same time ignores the Analytical teacher who is a turnoff because she is not communicating comfortably to your teen. In both cases your teen may be unduly influenced.

Think of your own situations where you, a Driver, are interviewing an Amiable for employment. This person's record and qualifications are consistent with those of others being considered. Do you hire based upon your STYLE comfort, or upon looking at the Flexibility potential of the person, or how he or she would mix with others on your staff?

What about that Analytical customer, who drives you, an Expressive, to frustration by continually asking for information and not making a decision. Do you stop calling on him, or start pushing by applying pressure to decide? Either way you may be defeating your objective of earning his business.

Think about the Expressive who looks impulsive and emotional to your Analytical eyes. Do you hold her up for promotion because you think she can't manage effectively?

Are you, an Amiable, taking your Driver boss or coworker personally—thinking he just doesn't care when in reality he does but his comfort influences him to be on task and move quickly?

We are prone, at times, to:

SEE   →   **JUDGE !** →   **REACT !**

We take STYLE personally and are emotionally hurt. We may think someone is intelligent or flighty or indecisive when they may not be—but their STYLE tricks our perception and we may make an error by listening when we shouldn't or not listening when we should.

How do we stay in charge of ourselves and read others more accurately? An effective way is to not judge too quickly. As human beings we tend to read the book by its cover—judge and decide by first impression, or limited information. This is not fair to others and not fair to ourselves. We make mistakes because of it.

Another way not to be controlled by STYLE is not to react too quickly. We all have beliefs and feelings, and some effort needs to be exercised to contain them before we react. Remember, too, not to be unduly influenced by our own STYLE. How many times in life have we formed near instantaneous likes and dislikes of others which were then proved wrong?

A LifeSTYLE STRATEGY

Applying the model on page 97 will serve us much better, and help us to read the real person and his or her real intentions, allowing better personal decisions on our part.

Practicing this process will trigger thinking. The more we think about things the more we can make realistic decisions about others and what is happening to us.

This is another major aspect of Flexibility.

How Do We
Get Them To Respond?

We earn the right to have our needs met when we meet the needs of others.

The more we are not controlled by the STYLE of others, the more we can do the things we need to do to gain positive response.

STYLEBYTE

Not being controlled by STYLE is a personal responsibility. It is still up to us to accept or reject the influence and attempts to control others exert.

The greater our flexibility the less our own STYLE comforts exert control over our behavior. We pressure ourselves with a great deal of influence through our STYLE.

Some use their STYLE as an excuse to not do the appropriate thing. They consider themselves locked into their behaviors and unable to do anything about them.

The Amiable who believes they must accept what others hand them on the job, or in their personal life, may say after the STYLE training, *"I'm an Amiable—so what can I do? I don't have any control at (insert your own: work, home, school, church, temple, with parents, significant other, etc.)."*

This Amiable is using their STYLE as an excuse. They may also have said things like this before STYLE training, but now they have a justification for their lack of the *doing* that which would help them to regain control of themselves and their circumstances.

What is really happening is they are not motivated, or too fearful to *do* (take the responsibility and change their behavior).

A Driver who says, *"So I told them if they didn't do it they wouldn't have a job tomorrow. I'm a Driver that's what Drivers do."*

This Driver probably does not want to use the energy to be more Flexible and is using STYLE as the excuse. He or she didn't want to use the energy before STYLE training—and they still don't want to do it now.

STYLE knowledge doesn't stop these people from not being Flexible, or more in charge of themselves, but it does give them more tools to make the change needed if they wish to do it.

Taking one's STYLE as an excuse for inappropriate behavior is as inappropriate as any other excuse; what makes it worse is that the time they spent learning more about how to do things better has been wasted.

If one really wants to take more control of themselves, not others, to do the things they need to do to get more of what they want, they need to use STYLE knowledge more and *do* more.

Remember, there are several places we have discussed thinking in this book. Thinking is so critical to moving from *knowing to doing.*

Think about how you are unduly influenced by others.

Think, as well, about how you are unduly influenced by yourself and your STYLE comforts.

It's up to you to change this pattern, and you have some additional tools now to do it. These STYLE tools of profiling others—Flexibility, and LSQPA—can give more assurance that the road to change the things you need to change isn't as fearful or difficult as it may have looked.

Good Luck!

Chapter Fourteen

STYLE MAKES A DIFFERENCE IN THE WORLD

"The Bottom Line. This One's Not Just For Drivers."

STYLE doesn't make events, it influences the decisions that make events. **This is extremely powerful.** How a person gathers data and—

- the amount of data
- the speed of the decision
- the speed of the action
- the personal motivation
- the habits and comforts

—are all at play during the decision making process and contribute to the decision.

A Russian leader, a Driving Expressive, leaps upon a tank in Red Square, faces down the Soviet army winning them over—and the world changes.

An American President, an Amiable Analytical, orchestrates a handshake between the leaders of Israel and Egypt—and that part of the world becomes safer.

A Nazi dictator, an Expressive, rises to power, bringing pride to an entire nation—and plunges the world into its most terrible chapter.

Please understand; it's not that STYLE made them do this. They decided to do it. Of the factors that influenced their decisions, however, their STYLE is also accountable. The quality of the decision and how resources are used—for good or evil, is based upon the person's morals, values, education, intelligence, emotional state and many other factors which go much deeper than STYLE.

Certain actions, however, are influenced by STYLE, and if not totally predictable, are possible to anticipate and prepare for.

The preceding examples are world events—concerning world leaders—but what about our own personal events? Are they any less influenced? Whether we are conscious of it or not, how is STYLE influencing our relationships and situations?

- a parenting problem we may have

- a customer who is hard for us to read

- a coworker we just don't get along with

- a significant other we may be breaking up with

How might a greater understanding and skill at using Flexibility affect these situations so they have positive endings?

If we are not aware of this factor, we are not using Flexibility to its full potential, and you and I may be unduly influenced by our STYLE or the STYLE of others. That would be giving up some of the little power and control we really have. **In this age of information, we cannot afford to be without STYLE information.**

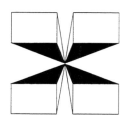

How Do We Get Them To Respond?

To paraphrase Abraham Maslow, *"People do things for their reasons, not ours."* STYLE tells us very quickly some of the *whys* people do things.

We get others to respond if we understand more of the *whys* and demonstrate that understanding through Flexibility. Then, as others are on their way to creating what to them are world class events, they may stop long enough to respond by helping us make ours.

STYLEBYTE

It isn't that STYLE *could be* a factor in our lives—it IS a factor in our lives, whether we recognize it or not.

Style is always with us—we take it wherever we go—we show it to everyone—it is one of the ways people judge us. It is always part of the human dynamic of interpersonal communication.

Knowing STYLE and using Flexibility can enhance the quality of our lives by building trust, stimulating communication, and influencing the decision-making process. This can position us to have greater cooperation from others. Think of what that means when influencing your customers, coworkers, family, boss, and significant other.

How much more can we do and be with STYLE working for us?

A BRIEF HISTORY OF STYLE

"Its been around for a long time."

Many times when someone is newly introduced to STYLE, they ask the question, *"Is this some new fad?"* People want to know if STYLE is something dreamt up to be different, have its fashion run, and be gone by next year's craze.

This is not true in the case of STYLE.

STYLE Technology has been in use for training in interpersonal skills, management, leadership, team management and leadership, sales, TQM, customer service, parenting, etc. for many decades. A host of training companies, some world wide in scope, have a version of the program.

TRAINING MAGAZINE has published numerous articles about STYLE. In one, no less than 15 companies were charted showing how they all had STYLE related courses.

Before STYLE was used in modern training programs, Swiss psychiatrist Carl Jung studied behavior and made pioneering STYLE type conclusions.

Other psychologists and behavioral scientists have refined and gathered extensive data on *behavior analysis, matrix management, and typing.* Names like Merrill, Reid, Marston, Geier, Atkins, and Colby are well known as contributors to this and similar technologies.

Something very much like STYLE—Hippocratic Doctrine on temperaments—was expressed in the second century.

In the middle ages conditions of the mind were believed to be caused by fluids of the body. The fluids produced the four types of personality—sanguine, bilious or choleric, melancholic, and phlegmatic. Some still use these terms as descriptive of human behavior.

STYLE has been around for a long time, and as more data is collected, will continue to enhance and contribute to our understanding of ourselves and others for the future.

A GLOSSARY OF STYLE

AMIABLE   A STYLE type description characterized as *Emote* Reactive and *Ask* Assertive.

ANALYTICAL   A STYLE type description characterized as *Control* Reactive and *Ask* Assertive.

ASK   A descriptive label for the left half of the *Assertiveness* dimension. An *Ask* Assertive is more comfortable *Asking* than *Telling*.

ASSERTIVENESS   The degree to which a person attempts to control the thoughts and actions of others. Depicted by being either *Tell* ASSERTIVE or *Ask* ASSERTIVE.

COMFORT   A state of emotional well being. Feeling of satisfaction, or emotional safety.

CONTROL   A descriptive label for the top half of the *Reactiveness* dimension. A *Control* Reactive is more comfortable in *not* showing outward emotion.

DRIVER   A STYLE type description characterized as *Control* Reactive and *Tell* Assertive.

DEFENSIVE BEHAVIOR	Each STYLE has a unique way of exhibiting *Fight* or *Flight* behavior. They are: **Driver**—Demand **Expressive**—Attack **Amiable**—Give-in **Analytical**—Avoid
EMOTE	A descriptive label for the bottom half of the *Reactiveness* dimension. An *Emote* Reactive is more comfortable in showing emotion outwardly than a *Control* Reactive.
EXPRESSIVE	A STYLE type description characterized as *Emote* Reactive and *Tell* Assertive.
FIGHT / FLIGHT	Approach or avoid conflict. Two major forms of defensive behavior.
FLEXIBILITY	The amount of effort, or observable energy, a person expends in meeting the interpersonal needs of others. A skill and a choice—this is the major concept of STYLE technology, and our Flexibility is critically responsible for interpersonal success.
FLEXING	A strategy / action of temporarily modifying behavior for using Flexibility with each STYLE.
LSQPA	A skill set for dealing with defensive behavior in others. **L** = Listen / **S** = Share / **Q** = Question / **P** = Present / **A** = Ask.

LifeSTYLE STRATEGY

To not just *see and react*, but to *Observe, Think, and Decide*" instead.

PROFILE

A instrument tool, which may be computerized, to help determine your STYLE and Flexibility as seen by yourself or others. Profiling by others is much more accurate than self profiling.

QUADRANT

An intersection of the Assertiveness and Reactiveness dimensions resulting in the four major STYLES.

REACTIVENESS

The degree a person tends to control the outward expression of feelings, reactions, and emotions. Sometimes called *Responsiveness* or *Objectivity*. Depicted by being either *Control* REACTIVE or *Emote* REACTIVE.

SELF MANAGEMENT

An important aspect of Flexibility. It is using patience or not giving into the natural comfort of one's STYLE which may be inappropriate in dealing with a given situation, e.g., a *Tell Assertive STYLE* not giving into the natural inclination of *Telling*, even though it is comfortable.

STYLE

A mixture of habits and conditioning, which is exhibited through behaviors that affect our comfort. STYLE is illustrated through the dimensions of ASSERTIVENESS and REACTIVENESS.

STYLE MAP   A matrix which indicates where Assertiveness and Reactiveness intersect to form each STYLE. The map is also used to show characteristics of each STYLE and how to Flex to them.

SUBQUADRANT   A further break down of STYLE Reactiveness and Assertiveness dimensions. There are four subquadrant types for each major quadrant of STYLE.

TELL   A descriptive label for the right half of the "Assertiveness" dimension. A "Tell" Assertive is more comfortable "Telling" than "Asking".

Appendix C

ADVISOR LIST

The *Advisors* for this book include corporation executives, investment counselors, trainers, consultants, clergy, sales professionals, and teachers. They represent all four major STYLES and are proud of it. They also are highly Flexible and quite successful in their fields, which proves once again—STYLE does not determine one's success—the person and their Flexibility determine their success.

All advisors leant their experience, knowledge, skill, and expertise freely and without question to me. If the reader gains by reading this book, then, they and myself have the advisors to thank.

I have learned about STYLE through the efforts of these people. Some were my teachers, some were my students, all are successful practitioners of STYLE. The key word for me in referring to them is "Respect". They are listed in alphabetical order:

Paul D. Anderson
Paul is Corporate Manager of HRD and Communications for Bankers Systems Inc. He is also President of his own consulting firm Total Development Concepts. A list of companies he has held management positions in training and HRD reads like a "What's What" in corporate North America. They include 3M Company, Northern Telecom, and Carlson Companies. He has nine years of organizational consulting, and 25 years of Human Resource Development and training experience to his credit. Paul has worked with several different behavior programs and instruments including Influencing With STYLE, DISC, Meyers-Briggs, and SIMA. Paul is an Amiable.

Ralph C. Colby

Ralph is author of the STYLE and Flexibility Indicator Instruments, considered by some to be the most accurate of their kind in the industry. This instrument has a history and data base accumulated since 1973. He is considered one of the gurus of STYLE. Ralph Colby's career spans many disciplines. A parish minister in New Hampshire, Ohio, and Minnesota—Ralph joined Wilson Learning Corporation in 1970 as Director of Education. While there he wrote training programs and managed the training staff. In 1973, Ralph co-owned Integro, a consulting and training company which he brought to the top 10% in industry size. He sold Integro to Carlson Companies, and became President of Purup North America, Inc. The company subsequently experienced accelerated growth due to Ralph's leadership. He left Purup in 1987 and is now an independent consultant and trainer. Ralph is a Driver.

Richard Cunningham

Richard conducts training and development in human services for one of the largest county governments in the United States. He has a master's degree in Business Education, is Leader Trained in Influencing With STYLE, and is versed in Meyers Briggs and DISC technologies. He possesses a master's level of ability to design training utilizing STYLE as a means of teaching team building, conflict management, and interpersonal communication. Richard is an Analytical.

George Daum

Vice-President of Sales for CAMAX Manufacturing Technologies, George has extensive experience in worldwide sales and sales management in the CAD/CAM software field. He has established and managed 3rd party distribution channels which include North America, Latin America, Europe, and the Pacific Rim. He applies his STYLE knowledge to peoples in all the countries involved and I have witnessed his high flexibility skill which he uses seemingly without effort. George is an Amiable.

Linda Hammond

After graduating from the University of Minnesota, Linda has built a career in hearing research, speech and language pathology, training, and has authored a book on FM Auditory Trainers for teachers, students, and parents. She has 21 years of experience in sales and is a regional sales manager in the hearing instrument field. She is leader trained in Influencing With STYLE and has been using the technology for 10 years in communication and problem solving with customers, coworkers, family and friends. Linda is an Expressive.

Lisa Jean Hoeft

Lisa Jean has been a Customized Training Facilitator for Southwestern Technical College. She now heads her own training company, Lisa Jean & Associates, She is a Certified Training Facilitator for many Zenger Miller courses as well as several other customer service and continuous improvement programs. She is a Master Leader Trainer for Influencing With STYLE. I have seen Lisa Jean take a training segment and by adding a creative experiential exercise, turn it into a learning event. She is very, very good at what she does. Lisa Jean is an Expressive.

Neil A. Levy

Neil has a BA and MA in Psychology, with a concentration in personality theory. He has been a Consulting Senior Manager for Touche Ross & Company, Vice-President for Genesco, Executive Vice-President for Eye Care Centers of America, Vice-President and General Manager for Doubleday Book Shops and Scribner's Bookstores, and President & General Manager for Telex Communications. I would go on, but I would be too envious of his credits. Of this friend, advisor, and teacher I will only add that I have learned, gained, grown from having known him. Neil is an Expressive.

Barbara Mattson

Barbara is a Senior Account Manager with Stevens, Foster Training. She has over ten years experience in training, sales, and consulting. She is certified in Influencing With STYLE and has consulted on its use as a communication tool with 3M Company,

Seagate Technology, Dayton Hudson, Ecolab, and many other organizations. She has traveled extensively internationally and has studied in Spain. Barb is an Expressive.

William R. Sather

"Willy" is a Vice-President for Dean Witter Reynolds. An investment counselor, he has great compassion and respect for people. His honesty and integrity only are matched by his love for his family. I have seen Willy use great skill in very difficult—high tension situations and respond with Flexibility and empathy for a person that others might become defensive with. He already knew how to use STYLE skills well before any formal training in the technology. Willy is an Amiable.

Ronald P. Strand

My association with Ron goes back to 1967. He has been my teacher, mentor, friend, advisor, and parent model. He has a master's degree in education, has been a teacher, trainer, consultant, and state education supervisor. Ron was with Wilson Learning Corporation for sixteen years as Account Manager (achieving top sales productivity awards) and Regional Sales Vice-President. Ron is now President of Stevens, Foster Training. Ron is an Expressive.

Irene B. Teske

Irene's achievements are many and continuous. She has a degree in Communicative Disorders, has been a special needs teacher, product manager, and is now a national Director of Sales. She has extensively used STYLE as a training, management, and sales vehicle for the people who work for her. These include sales professionals, managers, customer service and support staff—all of whom are under her leadership. I have witnessed Irene's ability to *apply* STYLE with customers, employees, coworkers and in many difficult situations. In my opinion, no one does it better. Irene is a Driver.

R. (Bob) Van Driel

Bob is Director, Continuous Improvement for the Feed Division of Land O'Lakes. He has thirty years experience in the training and development field. Not small accomplishments, he has established programs to teach immigrants to read and formed the training departments of two Fortune 500 companies. He continually points out the need to learn. In the time I have worked with Bob, I found him to add that rare touch of sincerity, dedication, and humanness to training and people. Bob is an Analytical.

My thanks also to my publisher and editor David Knutson—an Amiable, and my many associates and friends of all STYLES. If I have left you out of this list, please remember I am an Expressive and prone to make mistakes like that.

Appendix D

ABOUT THE AUTHOR

David L. Teske
Author of **WHAT IF THEY DON'T RESPOND? Four Approaches To Influencing People With STYLE**

David Teske began his work with STYLE Technology in 1968. After working with and using many STYLE methods, he authored his own courseware in 1974 by developing material included in a program for the Minnesota Technical College system.

He continued to enhance his STYLE knowledge while consulting with numerous companies and facilitating hundreds of STYLE seminars in management, sales, team building and customer service fields. In 1984, as a performance consultant for Wilson Learning Corporation, he facilitated their version of STYLE for several Wilson clients. From there Dave became Manager of Sales Training for Northern Telecom Incorporated. At Northern, Dave was responsible for the training of over 900 sales, sales management, customer service, and other sales support personnel—with STYLE being a central focus.

In 1986, Dave formed Training Advisors and published INFLUENCING WITH STYLE, a text and workbook. This work has gone through several enhancements and versions have been purchased by Northern Telecom, Telex Communications, Cenex/Land O' Lakes, 3M Company, CAMAX Manufacturing Technologies, The Federal Reserve Bank, Lutheran Brotherhood, Northrup King Company, Dayton-Hudson Corporation and other companies and organizations of all sizes.

At the time of publication of **WHAT IF THEY DON'T RE-SPOND?**, he has 27 years of experience in this field, and has trained others in STYLE from many different countries including England, France, the Netherlands, Japan, Germany, Russia, Canada, and the United States. Dave is an Expressive.

Appendix E

Bibliography

This not a complete bibliography, but will serve as a beginning for a more ambitious list.

Blood And Black Bile: Four-Style Behavior Models In Training Article, Training/HRD, O'Brien, January 1983.

Funny, You Don't Look Twoish Article, Esquire, Schwartz, March 1995.

Gregorc Style Indicator Instrument, The Learner's Dimension, Butler, Copyright 1984.

How Do They Manage? Article, AMERICAN WAY, Fletcher, October 1982.

Influencing With Style Courseware, Training Advisors, Teske, Copyright 1986.

Influencing With Style: Celebrate The Differences Courseware, Training Advisors, Teske, Copyright 1986, 1991, & 94.

Interpersonal Style Inventory Instrument, Colby, Copyright 1973. Teske Copyright 1992 & 95.

Myers-Briggs Type Indicator Instrument, Consulting Psychologists Press, Inc., Briggs/Myers Copyright 1943, 44, & 57.

Parents Should Know Kids Behaviors Styles Article, Star Tribune, Gardner, July 19, 1992.

Personal Profile System Instrument, Performax, Geier, Copyright 1977, Revised 1979.

Recognizing Social Style Effective Tool Article, Leib, The Denver Post Business, June 29, 1992.

Social Style Profile Instrument, Wilson Learning Corporation, Copyright 1975.

Style Awareness Training Instrument, Personnel Predictions and Research, Taylor/Merrill, Copyright Taylor 1964—Merrill and Taylor 1977, 85.

The Many Faces Of The Four-Style Grid Article, Training Magazine, November 1982.

To Motivate Others Try Versatility Article, Industry Week, Pascarella, 1982.

Typecasting Article, Star Tribune, Fuller, April 18, 1988.

What's Your Style? Article, Training, Lee, May 1991.

Every effort has been made for accuracy on the preceding list, if an oversight has occurred it was not intentional. The copyright and article dates are from the author's files.

HOW TO ORDER THE STYLE AND FLEXIBILITY REPORTS

The **INTERPERSONAL STYLE INDICATOR** computer generated **STYLE and Flexibility Reports** described in Chapter 9 are an invaluable source which indicate how others see your STYLE and Flexibility. They provide strategies showing how you can be more effective with relationships of all kinds and are available through **Stevens, Foster Training.**

WHAT YOU WILL RECEIVE

For each set of **STYLE and Flexibility Reports** desired, you will receive one packet containing instructions, questionnaires you distribute to those you desire to describe your STYLE, and reply envelopes for those selected by you to mail their completed responses directly to Stevens, Foster Training.

Stevens, Foster Training will process the completed questionnaires and return the completed STYLE and Flexibility Reports with explanation directly to you within 7–10 days of receiving the completed questionnaires. You can call us any time during the process to determine the status of the number of questionnaires we have received to date.

HOW TO ORDER

To order, send your name, address, and $85.00/ packet to:

Stevens, Foster Training Inc.
8500 Normandale Lake Boulevard, Suite 140
Bloomington, MN 55437

Call (612) 921-3982 or (800) 678-5558 for additional information. MN residents include 6.5% sales tax. Price is subject to change.